Revolution

ALSO BY

Russell C. Coile Jr.

The New Hospital

The New Medicine

THE GRAND ROUNDS PRESS®

Revolution

Russell C. Coile Jr.

WHITTLE DIRECT BOOKS

Charts: Carol Zuber-Mallison. Sources: page 29, estimates by the Health Forecasting Group, Santa Clarita, California (data from *InterStudy Edge*, January 1, 1991; HIAA employer survey, 1989-1990, Health Care Financing Administration, U.S. Department of Commerce, and American Association of Preferred Provider Organizations); page 33, Foster Higgins & Co., cited in *Business & Health*, November 1991, and estimates by the Health Forecasting Group, 1992; page 44, *Business & Health* special report, "Integrating Managed Care," January 1991; page 48, Ernst & Young and *Health Care Competition Week*, March 1992; page 49, Health Care Financing Administration; page 64, Russell C. Coile Jr., "Physician-Hospital Partnering" in *Hospital Strategy Report* , July 1992. Charts: Susan Brill. Source: pages 68, 69, the Health Forecasting Group.

The Grand Rounds Press: Martha Hume, Editor;
Ken Smith, Design Director; Susan Brill, Art Director

The Grand Rounds Press is a registered trademark of Whittle Communications L.P.

Library of Congress Catalog Card Number: 93-60347
Coile, Russell C. Jr.
Revolution
ISBN 1-879736-14-4
ISSN 1053-6620

The Grand Rounds Press

The Grand Rounds Press publishes original short books by distinguished authors on subjects of importance to the medical profession. During the coming year, Grand Rounds will present MD/2000, a special series of four books designed to help doctors make sense of the rapid changes occurring in the U.S. health care delivery system.

Grand Rounds Press books, which appear approximately every three months, are edited and published by Whittle Books, a business unit of Whittle Communications L.P. They reflect a broad spectrum of responsible opinions. In each book the opinions expressed are those of the author, not the publisher or advertiser.

I welcome your comments on this unique endeavor.

William S. Rukeyser
Editor in Chief

To my new family, Nancy, Amanda, Ariel, and Helen

Acknowledgments

Revolution is based on assumptions and predictions about the future of health care and medicine for which only I should be held accountable. But I am indebted to a number of sources for the ideas included in this forecast of medicine's outlook under health reform and managed care, including my colleagues Clem Bezold, Ph.D., Jeff Goldsmith, Ph.D., Leland Kaiser, Ph.D., Dan Lang, M.D., Stephen Shortell, Ph.D., Ross Stromberg, Dennis Strum, Ph.D., and Steven Valentine. I also wish to thank Clark Bell and Charles Lauer, Kathryn Johnson and Susan Anthony, and Elizabeth Zima for letting me air my views on medicine's future in their publications. A special thanks to Tim Hanson, Roger Foussard, Roger Green, and Doug Fenstermacker for testing these ideas "from the planet Mars" in their health system of the future in St. Paul, Minnesota. It was a pleasure to work with all concerned at Grand Rounds Press. Considerable thanks to my editor, Martha Hume, to Hillari Dowdle for early concepts of the project, to Pamela Lawson for the very thorough research services, to copy editor Barbara Roberts, and to Bill Rukeyser, who suggested the appropriate title for a book on medicine in transition. I'd also like to express my continuing appreciation for the support of Marie Spurling, my administrative assistant, who keeps my world turning. This book reflects many ideas of my wife, Nancy, who manages health care's human resources in a hospital in Southern California, the cradle of managed competition. Her patience and insight are much appreciated.

contents

A Shift in Perspective...

The flexibility to shift perspective is key to creativity and innovation. Sometimes a closer view or a different angle reveals a whole new truth. Sometimes it takes a step back to see the larger picture. At Marion Merrell Dow we are committed to an ongoing effort to discover, explore, and deal with reality by looking at our world from various and differing points of view.

MARION MERRELL DOW INC.

T he U.S. system of private health insurance has been in place since the Depression, when Blue Cross and Blue Shield were founded and private insurance companies first began to offer health coverage to individuals. Medicare and Medicaid, the public insurance systems designed to finance care for the elderly and the poor, are nearly 30 years old. During all of those years, American medicine's ability to prevent and manage disease has progressed to the point that U.S. health care is considered the best in the world.

Unfortunately it is also the costliest, and to some critics, the most unfair. Certain segments of the population—those covered by labor unions' Taft-Hartley insurance plans for example—have unlimited cradle-to-grave access to high-quality care at little or no cost to themselves. Other citizens, many of them fully employed, have little access to medical care of any kind because they cannot afford to buy health insurance.

This by-now-familiar description of the prevailing state of affairs has yielded a consensus among doctors, health policy experts, business and political leaders, and informed citizens that something must be done to fix the way we pay for and gain access to medical care. The question is what that something should be.

Research by Robert Blendon of the Harvard School of Public Health shows that the voting public is divided almost equally into thirds about which approach the United States should take to cure its health care system. One-third of those prepared to express an opinion favor pure managed competition, the theory advanced by economist Alain Enthoven of Stanford and the influential coalition known as the Jackson Hole Group. Another third of the public is leaning toward a single-payer, Canadian-style system. The other third favors a combination of tax subsidies and insurance-industry reforms similar to the approaches considered by the Bush administration.

Even physicians feel reorganization is inevitable. "I don't think there's any other way to fix the system," a New Hampshire family practitioner wrote in response to a 1992 *Medical Economics* poll that examined practicing physicians' feelings about national health insurance. "It may be inevitable," commented an Iowa ob-gyn, "but I don't feel it will solve many problems, just create new ones."

We can expect fundamental changes in the system within the next one to two years. Congress and the state legislatures will enact health care reform legislation that will alter the patient-physician relationship and the health care delivery infrastructure. Large businesses are shifting rapidly to managed-care plans that will reduce employers' health care costs. Whatever system eventually emerges, physicians and hospitals will be faced with declining or flat annual incomes while being obligated to continue to care for patients during a time of unprecedented turmoil and change.

Change will come hard for many of America's 600,000 doctors. The Clinton administration's American Health Security proposal barely mentions physicians' welfare—not surprising, since all denominations of organized medicine were excluded from Clinton's health reform task force, but not reassuring either. And while the debate rages in Washington, ordinary physicians in many areas of the country are under pressure to join ever-larger group practices, physician-hospital organizations, HMOs, and all manner of new structures without really understanding what they're joining.

Revolution is the first in a special series of four Grand Rounds

Press books designed to help physicians adapt to this new world. Readers will learn what shape the reformed system is likely to take, and what shape medical practice will take in response. Future volumes will offer more about how doctors can cope personally and professionally with a changed medical scene. Of course, no book can do more than help physicians reach their own decisions about how they will participate in the new system.

And no book can explain the future with absolute certainty. However, extrapolating from current trends, it is possible to describe the directions that the health care delivery system is likely to take in this decade. The conclusions I draw in the following chapters are based on nearly 10 years of research into the forces that shape our health care system.

On the brink of the reform era, the question for physicians is not what Bill and Hillary Clinton are going to do. The real question is, what is American medicine going to do to create workable solutions to the nation's health care dilemma? For without the medical profession's support and collaboration, health care reform may fail. And the alternative might be even worse—a complete government takeover of American medicine and health care early in the 21st century.

The time for physician leadership in managing national health care reform is now. The American medical revolution has begun.

CHAPTER one

PREDICT AND MANAGE

I magine it is the year 2000. To the strains of Vivaldi's *Four Seasons*, a young doctor scans the medical journals electronically, searching for a new way to treat a hospitalized patient whose condition has stubbornly resisted the clinical path that is conventionally followed in this regional health system. It is after midnight, but the medical library is still open. The doctor's computer is on line with the National Library of Medicine's electronic reading room, where every major medical journal is available. Following a hunch, the doctor finds three cases similar to her patient's.

The computer prints a copy of the pertinent articles while the physician switches quickly to the patient's medical record. Pressing a thumb against the electronic identification pad, the doctor is admitted to the community medical-record network, a paperless system that tracks the medical histories of 100,000 local patients. That afternoon's diagnostic results, MRI scan, X-rays, and consulting opinions come up automatically. Data from her patient's bedside monitor are only minutes old, fresh from the continuously watched telemonitor. The doctor orders a new course of therapy, discontinuing one medication and starting another. The order is electronically communicated to the nursing unit and confirmed within moments. The new therapy need not wait for morning.

For most of this century, American health care has been organized around acute illness. In the 21st century, medicine will refocus on maintaining health and minimizing the limitations of chronic disease. Technology will continue to be a driving force, but its emphasis will shift toward helping physicians predict and manage disease.

Two major changes in case management are occurring simultaneously: from invasive to noninvasive therapies, and from specialty care to primary care. New pharmaceuticals—some of them already in use—will increase medicine's advantage over surgery. Proscar (finasteride), for example, can be used to treat prostate swelling and avoid surgery. ACE inhibitors reduce the risk of heart attack and the need for heart surgery for patients with reduced heart function. A chemical analogue of fumagillin (an antibiotic derived from the fungus *Aspergillus fumigatus*) shows striking effects in limiting the growth of some tumors. And retinoic acid, an analogue of vitamin A, has the ability to shrink late-stage solid tumors when used in combination with interferon.

Many of these new therapies can be administered by the infusion of large-molecule proteins, which can be done on an outpatient basis in the hospital, doctor's office, or at home. The next wave of development will feature small-molecule equivalents that can be administered orally. Surgery in a glass will be practical medical therapy in the 21st century.

Most open surgeries in the 21st century will be performed endoscopically, predicts Stuart N. Davidson, director of the Center for Technology Assessment of the St. Joseph Health System in Orange, California, in *2020 Visions*, an account of the 1992 proceedings of the United States Pharmacopeial Convention. "[Surgeries] will combine the dexterity of a skilled operator; the imaging, data processing, and analytical capabilities of the computer; robotics; and a three-dimensional intracorporeal navigation system," he writes. "The surgical suite of tomorrow will look more like a catheterization laboratory." Much of tomorrow's surgery—perhaps 75 percent—is likely to be outpatient surgery or will involve short stays of one to three days in nonhospital recovery centers. Since much ambulatory surgery will involve easy, relatively painless techniques, primary-care physicians may do 30 to 50 percent of the work traditionally done by general surgeons and surgical specialists in hospitals.

For an illustration of the shift to nonsurgical approaches, look at current urological surgery. Transurethral prostatectomy (TURP) has already replaced most of the highly invasive techniques of open surgery once used to treat benign prostatic hypertrophy (BPH). Other endoscopic techniques, such as transurethral ultrasound-guided laser-induced prostatectomy and transurethral microwave thermotherapy, which are even less invasive, are likely to replace TURP. Ultimately, all surgical approaches to BPH may be replaced with pharmaceutical treatment and watchful waiting under physicians' supervision.

Gene therapy will also become a realistic way to manage patients by the year 2000. The complexities are huge, and replacing damaged and defective genes will still be in its infancy, but the first steps are already being taken, and the promise is immense. Imagine a woman with a genetic predisposition to arteriosclerosis. With genetic treatment, infusions of genetically altered endothelial cells might reline the blood vessels and restart the body's natural production of tPA. By 2000, these kinds of treatments will begin to move from experimental to accepted therapy, both for fetuses in utero and for adults.

The ability to grow genetically engineered proteins by the vat using the polymerase chain reaction (PCR) is propelling this genetic revolution. The first wave of genetically engineered drugs is already arriving. Two cytokines, EPO(erythropoietin) and G-CSF (granulocyte-colony stimulating factor), suggest the power and promise of applied biogenetics.

EPO is naturally produced in the kidney in response to altered blood levels of oxygen. The hormone travels to the bone marrow and triggers the maturation of red blood cells. The resulting increase in the erythrocyte count helps correct for anemia. G-CSF stimulates white blood cells to regenerate after bone marrow transplantation or whole-body radiotherapy for cancer.

PCR is also dramatically simplifying how molecular studies are conducted as well as what questions can be answered with fairly simple lab techniques. Given a few molecules of DNA, researchers can now identify pathogens with conventional laboratory instruments at a relatively low cost. A complementary technique, ligase chain reaction (LCR), is being developed and may replace PCR by 2005. LCR is a one-step approach that amplifies the DNA sample while simultaneously detecting the sought-after substance.

In another technological improvement, high-speed imaging devices will grow ever sharper and more cost-effective. Ultrasensitive imaging devices will enable doctors to visualize the early signs of a disease much sooner. The result: pinpoint diagnosis and early intervention. Leading the way among such techniques is magnetic resonance imaging (MRI), which uses magnetic fields to reconstruct images of soft tissues and to detect malignant growth. A powerful diagnostic device, MRI will also guide surgery, even that using robotics. Advances in MRI's scanning speed, along with improved contrast agents, will result in high-resolution in vivo brain studies that were previously impossible. Magnetic resonance angiography probably will replace conventional angiography.

Another technique, magnetic resonance spectroscopy (MRS), will provide a complete biochemical analysis noninvasively. Combined with MRI, it will furnish both anatomic images and spectroscopic analysis of breast tissue. Thus, radiologists will be able to determine both the biochemical composition of suspected tumors and the probability of malignancy. This combined imager and chemical analyzer will be the centerpiece of the ambulatory-care imaging centers of the future, predicts Stuart Davidson.

Biomechanics will help improve the quality of life for the chronically ill. Someday high-risk patients might be continuously monitored with implanted biosensors linked to a regional medical-alert system that could dispatch a home-help team when a patient's condition deteriorates. Still in the experimental stage, biosensors are computer chips constructed of a variety of substances, synthetic and natural, that are intended to function as minilabs to provide many of the body-fluid and tissue analyses once done only in clinical laboratories. Sugar beet cells, for example, can be used to detect tyrosine, a cucumber leaf to detect cystine, and rabbit liver to detect guanine.

Biosensors may operate on their own, as early-warning monitoring stations, or in tandem with drug-dispensing devices. Once implanted under patients' skin, they can continuously report physiochemical and electrochemical data to a readout device or computer. These inexpensive monitors will eventually be available for virtually any disease; they'll be used in the care of the chronically ill in the hospital or at home. The primary-care office is the most likely home base for telemonitoring of biosensors, since primary-care practitioners will oversee the health of patients under managed-care contracts.

Technological advances and the ability to predict the course of a patient's health will enable medicine to take a more active stance in disease prevention in the 21st century. Genetic profiles will provide detailed information on patients' genetic weaknesses, and that information along with family histories will allow doctors to predict patients' health for decades ahead. Many people will be aware of their risk of chronic disease well before any symptoms emerge. Genetic serum markers will be used for mass population screenings and as clinical indicators in the long-term management of individual patients. Already, specific serum markers have been discovered for juvenile-onset diabetes and for some forms of prostate cancer and ovarian cancer.

Spurred by technology and such economic incentives as capitated payments and risk-sharing between health plan and doctor, physician gatekeepers and case managers will practice anticipatory medicine. Physicians at medical workstations will use diagnostic software to pinpoint problems, then manage patients by computerized care maps. Every hospital, large medical group, and health system will have its own practice guidelines and clinical protocols. Automated diagnoses will provide a computerized second opinion to the primary-care practitioner on when and how

A Shift in Perspective...

Marion Merrell Dow Works Locally...

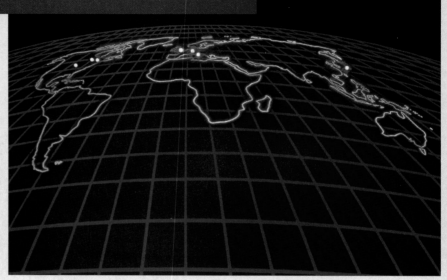

Marion Merrell Dow Works Locally but Thinks Globally

Around the world, Marion Merrell Dow research centers are home to hundreds of physicians and scientists whose curiosity and joy of discovery are nurtured in an atmosphere of freedom, openness, and informality. In Cincinnati, Kansas City, and Indianapolis...in Strasbourg, France and Gerenzano, Italy...in Winnersh, England and Hirakata, Japan–local Marion Merrell Dow associates look for innovative approaches and new perspectives in pharmacology. At each local facility, the view is global.

MARION MERRELL DOW INC.

to treat and whether to refer the patient to a specialist.

Computers will also allow doctors to develop long-term plans to optimize each patient's health. Medical breakthroughs will occur throughout the 1990s as the Human Genome Project maps the entire human genetic structure, working toward its goal of identifying all 100,000 genes by 2005. Researchers are steadily unraveling the keys to the 4,000 single-gene diseases and to complex health problems like cancer and diabetes, which are the result of multigene defects. By the turn of the century at least 1,500 to 2,000 single-factor diseases will have been linked to a specific pattern of genetic damage. The potential for health improvement in millions of Americans is enormous.

Since changing one's lifestyle has the greatest potential to reduce health risks, physicians may eventually spend 30 to 50 percent of their day counseling patients. But computerized health programs can raise health levels only if patients cooperate. Will President Clinton defeat his lifetime weakness for fast foods? Or does he "jog to eat"? The president is not the only one with unhealthy behavior. It will be tough for doctors to motivate every patient to live to his or her highest health potential.

Doctors will need incentives to increase compliance. For healthy people, lower health care premiums and reduced out-of-pocket copayments and deductibles could be the rewards. Cold cash would work too—employers might share the savings with employees whose personal health costs are low. When incentives are not enough, patients could be punished for their unhealthful habits with higher health care premiums and bigger copayments. Smokers are an especially inviting target, as are problem drinkers. Noncompliant patients with chronic conditions like heart disease and diabetes also merit special attention; they are time bombs waiting to go off in costly and life-threatening acute attacks. High-risk pregnant women might become the focus of a national campaign.

Of course, none of this means that disease will be banished. If today's researchers are correct, AIDS will still be a global epidemic with little hope for a real cure in the year 2000. There might be a vaccine, at least in clinical trials, by the end of the decade, but reports from the Salk Institute on early results of a vaccine approach were given little credence by researchers at the World Health Organization's 1993 Conference on AIDS.

Prevention may do more to slow the spread of AIDS. The World Health Organization, which estimates that 30 million to 40 million people worldwide will be infected with the human immunodeficiency virus by 2000, is mounting an international effort to spur preventive action, especially in the less-developed countries of Africa and Asia. The organization believes that investing $1.5 billion to $2.5 billion in an intensive campaign could result in long-term savings of $90 billion in direct and indirect costs by the end of the century.

In the United States, teens and young adults may be the population sector most at risk for future infection. AIDS has become the leading killer of young adults in 64 cities, according to a report by the Centers for Disease Control and Prevention. And although in the U.S. deaths due to AIDS had topped 180,000 by 1993, the disease has not yet peaked, says Dr. Sten Vermund of the National Institute of Allergy and Infectious Diseases. "Unless there is a substantially expanded national prevention effort," he says, "transmission by teens and young adults guarantees the continuation of the epidemic."

AIDS will not be the last new or previously unidentified disease we will encounter. The appearance of entirely new diseases is possible; more likely, we will find more subsets of existing diseases. In the spring of 1993, for example, "killer virus" headlines sent health authorities and physicians scrambling to uncover the cause of a mysterious ailment that had rapidly killed more than a dozen teenagers and young adults, mostly American Indians in the Southwestern U.S. Eventually, the cause was traced to a rodent-borne member of the hantavirus family, and not to a new disease. Scientists believe it is a member of a set of globe-trotting viruses found from Seoul to Baltimore that may have been carried by rodent stowaways on international flights from Asia.

Multidrug-resistant (MDR) strains of disease may turn out to be even more vexing. The tuberculosis bacillus, loosed once again, is rapidly becoming resistant to traditional treatment. The multidrug-resistant mycobacterium lacks a single gene that makes it vulnerable to treatment. And other genes that cause MDR in other pathogens will surely be discovered. To combat them, an MDR-gene inhibitor may someday be developed to reduce or block the genetic MDR weakness.

The advances outlined in this hopeful forecast of high-tech potential can occur only if costs are successfully addressed. Who will pay for this brave new world of medicine? This is already a $900 billion question, and if costs are not brought under control, America could spend $1.5 trillion on health and medical care by 2000. The proliferating use of sophisticated medical technology, which some health-industry critics blame for up to 50 percent of health inflation, has been encouraged by the U.S. system of insurance. Because most insurance plans cover virtually all patient costs, we get the "restaurant check syndrome," says Stanford economist Victor Fuchs. When everybody shares a common check, he explains, "you go out with a crowd to a nice restaurant and suddenly everybody develops a taste for lobster and baked Alaska." Fuchs is skeptical of medical technology's ability ever to be cost-efficient. "For every one [new technology or drug] that winds up saving money, 10 wind up increasing costs," he says.

For example, tPA, biogenetics' first major drug, stunned all major health plans and government programs with a price of $2,200 per dose when it was introduced in 1987. Nonetheless, hospitals still spent $188 million on the clot-dissolving heart drug in the first year. This may not happen often in the future. Today costly treatments such as autologous bone-marrow transplants are frequently rejected by payers as "experimental" simply because of the $100,000 to $250,000 cost per patient.

If health care technology is to realize its promise in the 21st century, two types of breakthroughs must occur. First, technological advances must meet the test of monetary efficiency: do they reduce the overall cost of care in an illness cycle or patient's lifetime? Second, biomedical and pharmaceutical advances must be priced over a product's life cycle of at least 17 years; manufacturers can no longer expect to recover developmental and other costs, plus a profit, in less time than that. They must invest in the future and demonstrate a socially responsible attitude toward profits.

Under national health reform, HMO committees and tough-hearted medical directors will scrutinize expensive diagnostic and therapeutic techniques for cost comparisons among treatments. Doctors will be told how much their prescribing decisions are costing the patient and the health plan. Computerized performance profiles will compare physicians' costs and outcomes of treatment with those of their peers. When there is a choice of drugs, doctors will have to defend their choice of a more expensive remedy. Practice guidelines and treatment protocols will also influence treatment decisions. Over the next 10 years, physicians will become more disciplined in their use of technology, knowing that their practice patterns will be under continuous review.

Quality will motivate treatment decisions as well. Beginning in 1994, the Joint Commission on the Accreditation of Healthcare Organizations will require hospitals to monitor and report clinical outcomes to maintain their accreditation. Large medical-care systems like Kaiser in California already conduct their own research, evaluating the costs and outcomes of new technology. The Park Nicollet Medical Center of Minneapolis also conducts clinical trials for technology evaluation and actively monitors the outcomes of its care.

Managed care—not national health reform—will squeeze high technology. The definition of minimum health benefits under national health reform will place some limits on coverage, though there will be no explicit exclusions for high-tech procedures; practice guidelines will be encouraged but not made mandatory. However, large self-insured employers, exempt from participation in purchasing alliances, will impose specific exclusions for high-cost procedures like bone-marrow transplants, and regional networks will develop internal practice guidelines and clinical paths that encourage low-tech diagnostic and therapeutic procedures. Formularies for both drugs and medical devices will limit physicians'

A Shift in Perspective...

At Marion Merrell Dow We Look
Beyond Science and
Technology...

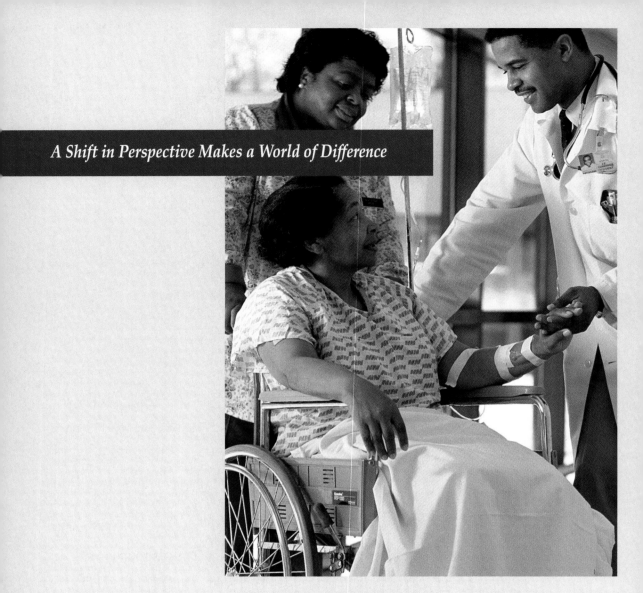

At Marion Merrell Dow We Look Beyond Science and Technology...Our Vision Is of Humanity

Wherever our research takes us, we never lose sight of its ultimate goal–improving the human condition. Alleviating pain and suffering. Improving the quality of life. Enabling the disabled. Extending the span of health and vigor. When we look at a molecule with a shift in perspective, we see a human being.

MARION MERRELL DOW INC.

MISAM615/B2179

access to brand-name pharmaceuticals. Gatekeepers will limit what medical subspecialists can do for their patients.

Despite the clamor over rationing that these developments might raise, it may not be the contentious arena doctors fear. Big regional health networks like the Kaiser Health Plan have a patient base that is broad enough to allow the network to provide a wide array of services. "It will be a long time before we have to say, stop doing something [useful] for a segment of the population because it's too expensive," says David Lawrence, the physician-CEO of Kaiser's parent foundation. On the other hand, Kaiser limited the use of a high-visibility imaging agent that is 10 to 15 times more expensive than conventional imaging media, even though the new agent causes fewer adverse reactions. Dr. David Eddy of Duke University, the consultant who advised Kaiser in its decision to save $3.5 million with the lower-cost media, points out that Kaiser could use the savings to invest in disease-prevention measures, such as aggressively seeking out women who have not had Pap tests for cervical cancer. The reform era will see more health plans follow Kaiser's lead, cutting their spending on ultraexpensive high technology and investing instead in prevention and health promotion.

But the U.S. health care community has a long way to travel before it arrives at this new and better destination, and the journey will not be easy. While some tentative first steps have been taken, the trip begins in earnest as the nation prepares to debate the nature of the health care system it wants. Do Americans still believe that private industry, driven by the profit motive, is the means of creating technological and pharmaceutical innovations? Do we believe that the government bureaucracy can be trusted to administer a system as essential as health care? Is access to health care an inalienable right that should be guaranteed by government? Do Americans believe that we are obligated to care for those who cannot care for themselves? If so, how much are we willing to pay? Will voters accept a change that might mean some people will pay more for health care than they do now while having a more limited choice of the physicians they can patronize? Is the country willing to take a chance on an untested system like managed competition merely in the hope that it might slow down cost increases? Do we have any choice in the matter at all?

Perhaps most important, what will physicians do to help solve this problem? The following chapters examine ways that physicians can make change work for them, rather than against them. The bright future awaits only those who are prepared to seek it out.

CHAPTER two

FORECAST: REFORM

T he private practice of medicine will still exist in the year 2000, and medicine will continue to be one of the highest-paid of America's professions. But how physicians practice and are paid will be radically different. The United States can no longer afford its health care system. In 1993 total spending for health care will exceed $900 billion—or 14 percent of the gross domestic product. Yet millions of people remain uninsured, effectively cutting them off from access to the health care system. As a result two powerful forces have combined to create fundamental change.

The first is pressure for reform in the public sector, which is stronger than it has been for three decades. Federal spending on Medicare and Medicaid in 1992 was $200 billion—14 percent of the federal budget. And the individual states' portion of the Medicaid bill is growing at a pace that threatens many state treasuries. Thus we are seeing a national effort to revamp the system. Several states, notably Florida, Minnesota, and Vermont, have already acted, and many others are drafting new legislation. In 1993 the Clinton administration was pushing the biggest reform effort of all—its American Health Security proposal. Although hardly anyone expects the Clinton plan to pass intact, some kind of reform, possibly a combination of state and federal legislation, will be set in place, probably by 1994 or '95.

The second force for restructuring comes from the private sector, where large employers, faced with ever-rising premiums for employees' health insurance, are trying to stop cost increases by taking independent action. Many are negotiating health care contracts with provider organizations that can implement money-saving managed-care programs. In fact, the managed-care system is poised for a nationwide introduction over the next five to seven years even if national health reform is not passed. So far this trend is strongest in California, Minnesota, Maryland, and Massachusetts, but it is spreading rapidly.

The structural centerpiece of both the Clinton health-reform proposal and some private-sector programs is managed competition, the policy that Alain Enthoven originally recommended to Carter administration health care reformers in 1977. As expanded by Dr. Paul Ellwood, the founder of the Jackson Hole Group, managed competition would create a wholesale marketplace for health care. Large purchasing groups organized by employers and the state and federal governments would contract for the services of regional health care networks. These networks, organized by groups of physicians, hospitals, and insurance companies on a regional or statewide basis, would compete for consumers. State agencies might oversee the competition, and the states might be given the power to set their own benefit levels and to combine Medicare and Medicaid funds to buy health care for the aged and the poor. Economists hope that such a restructuring of the system will hold medical-cost inflation to a level as low as the Consumer Price Index plus 1 to 2 percent.

But for managed competition to work, it is generally conceded that health care delivery must become *managed* health care delivery. The American health-insurance industry is already converting to managed-care approaches. Health-maintenance organizations (HMOs), preferred-provider organizations (PPOs), and managed-indemnity plans are replacing traditional unmanaged health insurance (see chart, opposite page). More than 28 percent of those

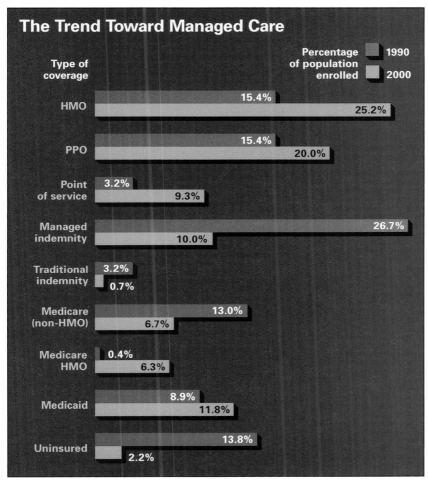

The Trend Toward Managed Care

Type of coverage	Percentage of population enrolled	1990	2000
HMO		15.4%	25.2%
PPO		15.4%	20.0%
Point of service		3.2%	9.3%
Managed indemnity		26.7%	10.0%
Traditional indemnity		3.2%	0.7%
Medicare (non-HMO)		13.0%	6.7%
Medicare HMO		0.4%	6.3%
Medicaid		8.9%	11.8%
Uninsured		13.8%	2.2%

Source: The Health Forecasting Group

This estimate of the future market shares of various forms of health insurance assumes that Congress will require employers to provide coverage for all workers and that states will use capitation payments to control costs.

covered by employer-sponsored health plans are already enrolled in an HMO, and managed-care plans are making inroads in every state and region. Within seven years, the majority of American consumers—70 to 80 percent of U.S. residents—will be covered by some form of managed-care plan, with premiums paid by employers, government, or the self-employed. Almost half will be in health-maintenance organizations and preferred-provider organizations, the rest in other kinds of managed-care plans. By 2000, managed care will no longer be an alternative delivery system; it will *be* the system.

Here's how the scenario is likely to play out:

National health reform, expected to be enacted in 1994, will require all employers to provide health-insurance plans for their workers. The biggest employers (those with more than 5,000 workers) are likely to be exempt and may contract directly with providers of health coverage. Smaller employers, the self-employed, and the government-funded uninsured will be pooled into large purchasing groups that will buy comprehensive packages of health care services from groups of physicians, hospitals, and insurance companies. By the time full coverage of all Americans is phased in, probably by 1998, charity care will have almost disappeared.

Health-insurance premiums will be based on community rates, to correct pricing practices that have favored large employers with low rates and discriminated against small firms. No one will be refused coverage because of a preexisting condition or catastrophic illness. Insurance coverage will be portable: employees will take their health plans with them when they change jobs or locations.

The minimum scope of benefits Congress will eventually approve is likely to resemble the standard Blue Cross/Blue Shield package that covers both hospital and physician services. Although the Clinton administration is pressing for inclusion of mental health benefits in the national plan, few extra health services—dental care for adults, cosmetic surgery, in vitro fertilization—are likely to be part of the minimum package. Abortion coverage will probably be included, despite Congressional controversy, but it will be subject to state restrictions, and no doctor will be forced to perform the procedure.

Reform may give the states substantial new powers over health plans. States might be responsible for certifying and regulating both purchasing groups (health alliances) and provider networks (health plans). Hospitals, physicians, and insurance plans organized into local and regional networks will have to demonstrate that they can provide the comprehensive benefits package specified by Congress.

The states might also gain federal permission to incorporate Medicare into state-level reform efforts. State Medicare programs could provide more benefits to senior citizens, such as coverage for prescription drugs, or they could pay doctors higher fees to encourage more doctors to accept Medicare patients. Several states have already applied for federal waivers to modify their Medicaid programs. So far, only Oregon's controversial "rationing" approach and Hawaii's play or pay plan have been approved.

Buyers and sellers of care in this system will set prices by capitation—a single premium for each patient that covers all services for a year. Although reform will preserve a role for traditional indemnity insurance, the new system will rely on HMOs and risk-sharing provider networks. Fee-for-service medicine, though still an option, will cost consumers a large deductible plus a 20 percent copayment. This is deliberate: reformers intend to drive consumers into more efficient HMOs and risk-sharing provider networks. Government will shift to capitation because current regulations have failed to stop Medicare or Medicaid price increases. Since providers can always outgame a micromanaged system, it is far easier for the government to put all doctors, hospitals, and health plans at full financial risk and let the provider side worry about controlling costs.

This can be accomplished while still paying lip service to preserving fee-for-service medicine; just look at the state of Minnesota. The MinnesotaCare reform plan, adopted by the legislature in 1992, will begin to regulate prices in July 1994 under a single-payer system for all physicians and hospitals that want to be paid on a fee-for-service basis. Minnesota physicians and hospitals fear that the state will set fee-for-service rates so low that providers will be driven into capitated plans. That, of course, is the whole idea.

Under this scenario America's health system should take on a new and more orderly pattern of stable relationships. Excess capacity in the system would be eliminated by self-disciplined management by the local networks. All physicians would select one network as their primary affiliation. Three- to five-year contracts would bind providers to the networks, and provider fees would be negotiated in advance. In capitated agreements, physicians and hospitals take the financial risks, and the inefficient or ineffective simply will not have their contracts renewed. When managed care is the norm, most state and local markets will have only a relative handful of large HMOs that will maintain long-term contracts with regional or statewide provider organizations.

The price of government-mandated reform will be $60 billion to $100 billion a year. Who will pay? Most of the funding will come from cuts in spending on Medicare and Medicaid, from sin taxes on cigarettes, and from businesses and their workers, in the form of payroll taxes and possibly, income taxes on benefit packages that are more generous than the government-defined minimum plan. Doctors will help pay because their fees will be lower and they will see more controls over utilization. Physician and hospital fees could be frozen beginning as early as 1995, as the government phases in its plan. Increases in physicians' incomes may not catch up with inflation in this decade.

All of this is good news for those who pay America's health care bills, but the new system will have a profound and unsettling effect on most physicians. Private fee-for-service medical practice, the only system many doctors have ever known, will be largely obsolete. America's five largest health-insurance companies—Aetna, Prudential, Cigna, MetLife, and Travelers—have pulled out of the Health Insurance Association of America and formed the Alliance for Managed Competition, betting there will very little traditional indemnity insurance in the near future. They expect that most traditional indemnity plans will have converted to HMOs or PPOs by the year 2000 and that few insurers will offer an unmanaged indemnity plan for health insurance at any price. Within the next five years, health-maintenance organizations will complete their domination of the health industry. The equation is Capitation + Primary Care + Purchaser Alliance = HMO Domination. Buyers of health care will shift 100 percent of the financial risk to providers.

Why HMOs? The answer is simple: among all forms of health plans, HMOs have been the most successful in moderating health

A Shift in Perspective...

Predictable.

Dependable.

Unique.

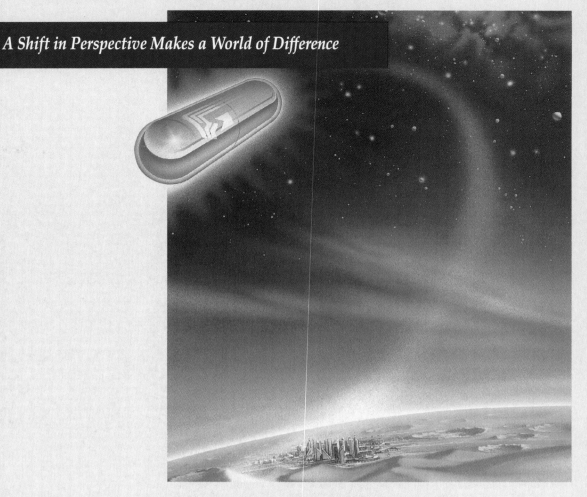

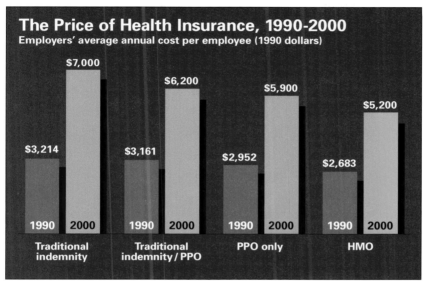

The Price of Health Insurance, 1990-2000
Employers' average annual cost per employee (1990 dollars)

	Traditional indemnity	Traditional indemnity / PPO	PPO only	HMO
1990	$3,214	$3,161	$2,952	$2,683
2000	$7,000	$6,200	$5,900	$5,200

Sources: A. Foster Higgins & Company; The Health Forecasting Group

HMO dominance of the health care industry seems unstoppable. While all medical costs will continue to increase, the costs of care for traditional indemnity plans will grow almost one-third faster than costs for HMOs.

spending and controlling medical utilization. Look at the price advantage HMOs offer employers (see chart, above). One example of the dramatic impact managed care can have on costs is to be found in hospital-use rates. In the 1970s, traditional indemnity health-insurance plans experienced hospital-use rates of 900 to 1,000 days per 1,000 subscribers, while HMOs used hospitals at a rate of 500 to 600 days. In the 1990s, managed indemnity insurance plans are expected to cut their hospital days to 300 to 400 days per 1,000 enrollees, while HMOs will slash their use rates further, to 200 to 300 days per 1,000 members.

With managed-care approaches, employers' costs for mental health care can also be reduced substantially. Between 1990 and 1992, HMOs' average length of stay for acute psychiatric conditions fell from 25.6 days to 19.8, according to the National Association of Psychiatric Health Systems. Nearly 90 percent of the association's members now offer limited hospitalization programs, up from 75 percent in 1990.

HMOs will win the market-share war with PPOs and managed indemnity plans because they provide more comprehensive benefits, predictable prices, less paperwork, and the fewest out-of-pocket expenses. As a result, health care utilization experts expect HMOs to enroll more than 50 percent of all Americans by the end of the '90s.

That, in turn, will lead to extensive consolidation among HMOs: the top 20 nationwide will have more than 60 percent of all members. Insurance companies, which already operate four of every 10 HMOs in the nation, may turn out to be major winners in this process. Large companies like Cigna, Aetna, Prudential, Metropolitan, and Travelers have the money to build national networks through internal growth and the acquisition of smaller plans. Mid-sized regional HMOs that may grow to be major national plans include U.S. Healthcare, PacifiCare, Foundation Health, Qual-Med, and Humana. And local HMOs like the Harvard Community Health Plan (Massachusetts), Group Health (Minnesota), the Group Health Cooperative of Puget Sound (Washington), and the Health Insurance Plan of New York could each increase their enrollment base to one million members or more.

All of this means that medical practice will consolidate as well. Doctors will practice in large, vertically integrated organizations. These groups of physicians, hospitals, and perhaps even providers of ancillary services such as medical laboratories and imaging facilities will gobble up huge numbers of patients (or "covered lives," as patients are called in the argot of capitated care), and the traditional hierarchy of medicine will be overturned in the process.

Remember the food chain model from Biology 101? The struggle for position in the medical-care-delivery food chain will be the battleground of health care markets in the 1990s. The world of medical status and physician reimbursement will turn upside down as large, well-organized primary-care medical groups with hundreds of thousands of capitated patients dominate. Once the least influential and most poorly paid of all, primary-care physicians will become the most powerful doctors in the system.

In 1991 about half (49 percent) of all cardiologists had net incomes of more than $200,000, according to a 1992 survey by *Medical Economics*. So did more than three-fourths of all cardiovascular surgeons. By comparison, only 8 percent of all family practitioners and 9 percent of general practitioners were in that upper-income bracket. Today Medicare's RB-RVS payment system and the impact of managed care are changing the balance of power. And a primary-care physician's cash flow from capitated patients can be substantial. At $8 per month per patient, a primary-care physician with a panel of 2,000 patients would receive $192,000 per year. The addition of a potential $2 per month gatekeeping fee would bring the total to $240,000. If this physician belonged to a group of 10 primary-care doctors, each with 2,000 patients, practice revenues would amount to $2.4 million. If the group had 100 doctors, revenues would hit $24 million.

Of course physicians in capitated systems are usually at risk for the costs of patient care, and this means that primary-care doctors will try to promote patients' health and keep them well over the long term, avoiding the need for hospitalization or for referrals to specialists. Primary-care gatekeepers will control such referrals, and they will monitor and reject clinically unnecessary procedures that specialists may provide. This will hurt specialists: studies show that as much as 40 to 50 percent of some specialists' practice volume consists of primary-care services.

Nonetheless specialists will be the next biggest fish in the food chain. To participate in managed-care networks, they will have to accept either a percentage of the capitated payment (called subcapitation) or a prenegotiated, discounted fee. Thus specialists will have to exercise self-discipline because they will risk financial losses if their costs go over budget. In California's predominantly managed-care marketplace, Blue Cross recently announced a 5 percent to 6 percent cut in fees for specialists serving the 1.8 million consumers covered by one of Blue Cross's managed-care plans. The action demonstrates how little control over prices specialists will have in a marketplace with a big purchaser. To protect themselves, specialists will have to restructure their practices by consolidating into single- or multispecialty groups, affiliating with hospitals and health care systems, or by becoming salaried staff physicians.

Hospitals may appear to be the biggest fish in the food chain, but they actually have the most to lose. The hospital share of the capitation budget will shrink from the current 38 to 42 percent of each dollar per patient per month to 30 to 32 percent by 2000. Hospitals might share a capitation risk or be paid per diem: there will be few volume guarantees in agreements between hospitals and primary-care medical groups. Also at a disadvantage will be university and public hospitals, whose costs are often 25 to 35 percent higher than those at comparable community hospitals. Many academic medical centers and public hospitals are not well networked with community facilities and physicians; some tertiary facilities have had an attitude problem because they have considered themselves superior to community hospitals. These teaching and public institutions risk isolation and substantial loss of revenues in the managed-care market.

Out at the end of the food chain—plankton—are the hospital-based specialists. The "RAP" physicians—radiologists, anesthesiologists, and pathologists—are the smallest and most vulnerable group. RAP doctors will be vendors to the primary-care physicians, forced to accept deeply discounted fees or a share of the hospital's payment. Unless RAP physicians organize on a multifacility basis to provide services to regional networks as partners, sharing capitation and abandoning fee-for-service, hospitals will give them a deal they can't refuse: Your contract is not renewed. Would you like to become a hospital employee, or leave?

By the end of the decade a wide-open choice of physicians and hospitals will be only a memory. Consumer choice will be limited to physicians and hospitals in participating panels and regional networks. On the other hand millions of patients will get more choice. Certainly the 37 million medically uninsured will have improved access to health care. Although the Clinton administration has promised to protect a fee-for-service option under national health reform, many Americans are likely to choose managed-care options because of their lower out-of-pocket costs or because they offer better benefits such as prescription drugs with minimal copayments. If that's so, patients will become cost-conscious shoppers. Patients will leave their doctor "for [a savings of] six dollars a month," warns urologist Roy Skoglund, of Roseburg, Oregon.

When the dust has settled, the patient-physician relationship will have a permanent new partner—the purchaser. That purchaser, whether an insurance company, an employer buying group, or the government, won't be a passive consumer. Buyers will be more involved than ever before in making decisions that have traditionally been the exclusive province of physicians.

CHAPTER three

THE HASSLE FACTOR

M anaged care has its good points. It saves money. It's more efficient. But managed care is a hassle for doctors, and it will continue to be so. The doctor-patient relationship under managed care will continue to be a treatment triangle in which a third party monitors the physician's every move, but soon the monitoring will come from the private sector as well as the government.

As physicians know all too well, America's third-party-review industry is booming. All purchasers of health care—insurers, managed-care plans, government, major employers—are hiring third-party-review companies to provide over-the-shoulder supervision of clinical practice. There were more than 200 private review companies in 1991, and their number is growing. Among the most successful are HealthCare Compare of Downers Grove, Illinois, Intracorp of Berwyn, Pennsylvania, and Private Healthcare Systems of Lexington, Massachusetts. Large insurers like Aetna, Metropolitan, and Prudential have developed internal review programs for prior approval and appropriateness review. Blue Cross/Blue Shield plans also have well-established review programs. State Medicaid programs operate a mixture of internal review programs backed by contracts with outside firms. The labor unions' health plans rely on private review companies such as ValueHealth and Health-Care Compare.

And it gets even more complicated. Health plans, hospitals, and government are beginning to shift from prior approval and post-treatment review to the continuous measurement of physicians' utilization patterns and quality of care. Systems like Iameter of Redwood City, California, and Atlas MQ (formerly MedisGroups), developed by MediQual Systems of Westborough, Massachusetts, gather data about physician performance and cluster it into as many as 500 diagnosis-related groups. Computers have made it possible to rapidly store, retrieve, and cross-reference almost any amount of quantitative information, and reviewers are learning to quantify previously unquantifiable information.

The only hope for relief from this ever-escalating micromanagement may come from outcomes research and management and continuous-quality-improvement systems (CQI, also called TQM, or total quality management). Even though some doctors decry outcomes management as "cookbook medicine," the field is beginning to yield hard scientific information on the one best way to treat many conditions. And CQI can translate heretofore intangible factors like patient satisfaction and efficient use of medical resources into hard data.

The goal of outcomes research is to reduce or eliminate regional variations in patterns of practice that are not based on scientific data. Outcomes management—case management based on the results of outcomes research—should enable physicians to standardize patient care to obtain predictable results in patients' health, functioning, and sense of well-being. It's important that physicians who are leery of outcomes management remember that doctors—not bureaucrats — are taking the lead in developing practice guidelines, and they will continue to do so. Ultimately the development of a professional consensus will give physicians a clearer sense of when to treat versus when to refer.

Take BPH, for example. Benign prostatic hypertrophy affects an estimated 75 percent of men by the time they reach age 80. Traditionally some 35 percent of those affected have undergone prostatectomy, the second-most-performed surgical procedure for Medi-care-aged men. In the past, individual primary-care physicians had varying thresholds for deciding when to refer such patients to urol-ogists for surgery. Now with support and research funding from the American Urological Association, academic urologists are de-veloping clinically sensible, evidence-based BPH practice guide-lines for both primary-care doctors and urologists. Guidelines like these, developed within the medical profession itself, should be more acceptable to doctors than rules promulgated from without by insurance companies or government agencies.

Outcomes management is still in its early days, of course. Right now the easiest things to measure are medical mistakes: undesired events like unexpected mortality, nosocomial infections, iatrogenic injuries, unplanned reoperations, unplanned readmissions within 31 days of discharge, unplanned transfers to the critical care unit, respiratory or cardiac arrest, and neurologic, nephrologic, vascu-lar, or pulmonary deficits present at discharge that were not pres-ent on admission. This is why CQI has entered the picture. As medicine travels up the learning curve of continuous quality im-provement, quality management will be able to shift its focus from measuring patient satisfaction to measuring physician competence and cost of care.

The spread of quality management is being spurred by new requirements of the Joint Commission on the Accreditation of Healthcare Organizations (JCAHO). The revised requirements are expected to go into effect in 1994 when the commission adopts a new manual and outcomes-based accreditation standards under president Dennis O'Leary's so-called agenda for change. O'Leary's plan, says a JCAHO spokesman, "makes the measurement and im-provement of health care organizations' performance the com-mission's top priority. One of the best ways to achieve this is through CQI." JCAHO-accredited hospitals will be required to record and report outcomes data on "perioperative indicators" and obstetrics beginning sometime after 1995. Data collection requirements for more services will be added each year until all major medical spe-cialties are included. And the Joint Commission has voted to be-

A Shift in Perspective...

At Marion Merrell Dow
We Show Our True Colors...

At Marion Merrell Dow We Show Our True Colors:
A Commitment to Government and Institutional Health Care

We have a clear understanding of the needs and expectations of government and institutional health care providers. We recognize that value begins–but does not end–with quality products. That's why we're committed to support programs that go far beyond your expectations–continuing education programs...cooperative research...technical consultation...product information hotlines...custom packaging...and patient education. All designed to assist you in the delivery of quality health care. We're Marion Merrell Dow.

MARION MERRELL DOW INC.

gin making its three-year accreditation surveys—although not outcomes data—public in 1995.

CQI can work, as illustrated by this example. In 1991 Long Beach Community Hospital, a member of the UniHealth system in Southern California, decided to attempt to shorten its length of stay for pneumonia patients. A team of clinical department heads and managers reviewed data on how cases were being managed in their own hospital and compared it with patterns of care in two sister hospitals. The Long Beach team determined that case management could be improved in three areas: antibiotic start time (which ranged from two to eight hours on one shift), timeliness of sputum collection, and timeliness of reporting sputum results. The medical staff and department of nursing developed a clinical path for pneumonia treatment that included these improvements, and the team created an educational program to inform all hospital staff of the changes. As a result, length of stay for these patients decreased from an average of 7.5 days in 1991 to 4.5 days in the first half of 1993.

Quality improvement can also give doctors and hospitals an edge in the marketplace. In the highly competitive Worcester, Massachusetts, area 52 percent of the 500,000 people are enrolled in an HMO. Over five years, three hospitals merged into one (Medical Center of Central Massachusetts); in addition, St. Vincent Hospital merged with the Fallon Community Health Plan, Worcester City Hospital became insolvent and was absorbed by the University of Massachusetts hospital, and two other hospitals converted to rehabilitation centers. Consequently the market has consolidated itself into three competing systems: the University of Massachusetts teaching system, the Fallon Healthcare System, and the Medical Center of Central Massachusetts.

Spurred by the need to be competitive, doctors at the 371-bed University of Massachusetts hospital are using CQI to reduce the utilization of services, slash patient-care costs, and improve clinical quality. Since 1987 the CQI program has cut the inpatient length of stay 34 percent, from 9.6 days to 6.3. The use of ancillary services has been cut as much as 40 percent for some patients. The university is using CQI to position itself as a provider of capitated care. As capitation becomes a major factor in physician-hospital payment, the financial incentives for clinically efficient medicine will be created.

On the other hand, once these systems are completely functioning, the practice of medicine will take place in an electronic fishbowl. Eventually every medical record will be accessible to payers, third-party-review organizations, and government. Computer programs will monitor physician performance in hospitals and offices. Every patient visit, lab report, X-ray, consultation, inpatient stay—the complete record of clinical treatment—will be computerized and continuously analyzed.

Computer profiles of physician performance will compare one doctor with others on a hospital staff, or with peers across the nation. These profiles will be used for privileging, payment, and continuous economic credentialing. Large health systems will be able to centralize their assessment of physicians' performance, using cost and outcomes measures to compare primary-care doctors and specialists throughout the system, so as to standardize quality and cost. Third-party payers, managed-care plans, and self-insured employers will use computer programs to screen out physicians whose costs of care or lengths of stay are consistently high.

Doctors have good reason to be nervous about economic credentialing. Although few hospitals will have the nerve to drop a physician from the medical staff for any reason other than lapses in quality, HMOs, PPOs, insurance companies, self-insured employers, and even government will reward or punish doctors based on their cost of care. Doctors will economically credential other doctors. Independent practice associations will counsel physicians whose costs are out of line and drop them from managed-care panels if they are not compliant. Hospitals will be looking closely at factors like lengths of stay, use of ancillary tests from lab and radiology, consultations, number of office or clinic visits for the same patient, procedures, and cost per day. These will all be evaluated and compared from doctor to doctor.

In 1992 Blue Cross & Blue Shield of Minnesota instituted a

pilot program that reimburses doctors and hospitals based on out-comes. If costs are high or lengths of stay too long, Blue Cross pe-nalizes providers by reducing their reimbursement.

Federal or state governments may also install quality monitor-ing systems for public programs. In fact two states already have them. Every acute-care hospital in Pennsylvania and Iowa must report both costs and outcomes of care to the state. The data are published in a series of publicly available reports that compare hos-pitals. In Hershey, Pennsylvania, the chocolate-maker Hershey Foods has developed a network of preferred providers using hos-pital outcomes data from the Pennsylvania Health Care Cost Containment Council as an indicator of quality. A self-insured company with 15,000 plan members, Hershey has also contracted with "centers of selected services" for certain high-cost and high-risk procedures such as transplants.

As primary-care doctors take capitated responsibility for man-aging a defined set of patients, they will tightly oversee the per-formance of other physicians and specialists who are treating those patients. This is called spreadsheet medicine—the management of the costs of care.

Prescription drugs are a case in point. The doctor's Rx pad is a license to spend. American physicians prescribe an average of $65 billion worth of drugs each year, says the American Pharmaceuti-cal Association, a figure that could soar to $150 billion to $200 bil-lion by 2000 if current trends continue. "Mix creep" is part of the problem, as newer, more expensive drugs replace older, cheaper formulations. But retail drug costs rose 80 percent between 1985 and 1992, and in the coming years, third-party payers will target physicians' prescribing patterns for continuous audit, and HMO-PPO panels may drop high-cost prescribers as preferred providers.

Primary-care gatekeepers will hold the keys to the pharmacy. Prescriptions for the most expensive drugs will likely require pri-or authorization, and virtually all third-party payers will soon have limited formularies that restrict choice and require substituting generics for brand names. This is already beginning to happen: the

1992 market for generic equivalents was $29 billion.

Formularies reduce drug costs (see chart, left), and there will be little arguing with gatekeepers and payers over generics or equivalents. HMOs will buy drugs wholesale, and doctors normally will be allowed to prescribe only the drugs in the HMO formularies. Soon the typical office sales call by a drug company representative will be obsolete. Drug company representatives who wish to make sales calls to physicians at Kaiser Permanente, for example, are required to wear special identification tags, and they are not allowed to recommend drugs that are not in the Kaiser formulary, or to give any gift—even pens—to doctors. A sales representative who incurs three violations in one year is barred from Kaiser for six months. In addition Kaiser pharmacists "counter-detail" physicians by educating them about the use of the drugs included in the formulary. As a result 96 percent of Kaiser physicians' prescriptions call for drugs listed in the formulary; 75 percent of those are generic equivalents.

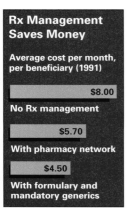

Rx Management Saves Money

Average cost per month, per beneficiary (1991)

$8.00
No Rx management

$5.70
With pharmacy network

$4.50
With formulary and mandatory generics

Source: *Business and Health*

Non-HMO doctors will also lose control over who fills prescriptions as insurers and managed-care plans contract with pharmacy chains for substantial discounts. Robert Navarro, formerly an administrator of Health Net, a California-based HMO, reports that some managed-care plans contract with only 30 to 50 percent of their communities' pharmacies in return for substantial discounts. Employers like Southern California Edison have set up in-house pharmacies and require employees and retirees to fill their prescriptions at the company store.

Drugs can also be bought by mail. Mail-order drug houses filled 90 million prescriptions in 1991. By 1995 an estimated 15 percent of all prescriptions will be delivered by the mail carrier; by 2000, mail-order pharmaceuticals may account for more than a fourth of the total. Merck, one of the largest pharmaceutical firms, is a believer in this trend: in 1993 it paid $6 billion to acquire Medco Containment Services, a huge mail-order pharmaceutical distribution firm.

In the end, control of prescribing patterns will be but one facet of primary-care physicians' power. Eventually all the data collected about the quality of medical care will become public, and primary-care physicians will be able to consult a national health care database to shop for consultants and hospitals, to evaluate the latest medical techniques for cost and effectiveness, and to predict the costs and clinical outcomes of treatment alternatives. But today there is a relative shortage of primary-care physicians. Will the nation have enough of them to run the new system? Where will we find them? Who will they be?

CHAPTER four

THE RISE OF PRIMARY CARE

I n a managed-care system, the primary-care physician—not the specialist—is the most powerful medical figure. As resource controllers and the first line of diagnosis and treatment, primary-care doctors will enjoy increased status and income. There will be bidding wars for primary-care doctors between HMOs, medical groups, and hospitals. Managed-care organizations will offer attractive salaries, bonuses, and reasonable work hours.

Consequently the number of doctors choosing to enter primary care is expected to expand. Growing demand from HMOs and groups for primary physicians could double the percentage of young doctors who choose a primary-care career.

How will this come about? After all, there is a shortage of primary-care physicians. Although the number of doctors in the U.S. has doubled—from 300,000 in 1970 to 600,000 in 1993—the real growth during most of that period has occurred in medical specialties and subspecialties. There has been no improvement in the primary care-specialty ratio. It is still 30-70 (not counting obstetricians), with specialists predominating in numbers of practices and in income. By comparison, the United Kingdom and Canada manage their physician supply by creating an equal distribution of primary-care doctors and specialists.

If the imbalance in the supply of primary-care physicians and specialists continues, some predict that the United States will be facing a physician glut in 2000. The U.S. has almost as many physicians to care for its population of 255 million as Canada, the United Kingdom, Italy, Japan, and Germany combined (population 344 million). In the 20 years between 1981 and 2000, the number of U.S. doctors per 100,000 population will have climbed from 208 to 247. The Graduate Medical Education National Advisory Committee predicts that the surplus of American physicians in 2000 will be 150,000. Other forecasts are even higher.

But in articles published in the late '80s in *The New England Journal of Medicine* and *Health Affairs,* health-services researchers Dr. William Schwartz, Frank Sloan, and Daniel Mendelson predicted that the physician surplus might actually be as small as 40,000 doctors, and that there could even be a shortage, of some 83,000 physicians. Their reasons include the following:

• The absence of accurate statistics on the number of active physicians. In 1993 far fewer than the 600,000 licensed physicians were actually seeing patients. In addition, a growing number of physicians are moving into administrative or other positions that do not involve patient care.

• The serious shortage of physicians to serve rural and inner-city communities.

• Physicians' practice of limiting patient loads by not accepting new patients or by reducing the number of days they see patients in response to declining reimbursement and rising practice expenses.

• The growing tendency among physicians to retire early because they are discouraged by the loss of clinical autonomy and the hassles of managing a medical practice. Many baby-boom physicians are likely to retire between 2000 and 2010, just as the rest of the boomers reach the over-55 age threshold and become higher risks for chronic disease and acute illness.

On the other hand, the rising numbers of women physicians should benefit primary-care group practices, since women tend to choose careers in family practice, pediatrics, and obstetrics. And women are especially likely to work for group practices or in staff-model HMOs so that they can balance the needs of family life with their careers. Meanwhile more medical students are being channeled into primary care, reversing the tide of young physicians opting for subspecialties. "Health of the Public," the reform program financed by the Pew Charitable Trusts and the Rockefeller Foundation, calls for a balance in medical education between high technology and people-oriented medicine. It proposes federally financed partnerships between academic health centers and community-based providers to prepare more students for primary-care careers.

One successful strategy hospitals and medical schools are using is to emphasize ambulatory care in residency training. Internal medicine residents at St. Joseph Mercy Hospital in Ann Arbor, Michigan, spend 30 percent of their time providing ambulatory care. That is approximately 20 percent above the minimum ambulatory-care requirement of the Accreditation Council on Graduate Medical Education. The hospital plans to have half of its residents on a primary-care training track within five years.

It's working. Since 1990 half of these internists have chosen to stay in primary care after residency, compared with only 35 to 40 percent of internists nationally. Another Michigan institution, Providence Hospital and Medical Center in Southfield, launched a similar program in September 1992. So did the Harvard Community Health Plan, where research and the education of residents focus on preventive health measures and ambulatory care for the health plan's 500,000 patients. In Detroit, the Henry Ford Health System is collaborating with Case Western Reserve University to train third- and fourth-year medical students. Medical students who stay with the health system through residency gain tuition subsidies.

The supply of primary-care physicians will also grow through economic forces. The integrated health systems of the 21st century will be built on a base of primary-care and multispecialty medical groups, because hospitals need such groups to survive in the managed-care marketplace (see chart, left). They need medical groups with a capacity to manage risk, since payment will be by

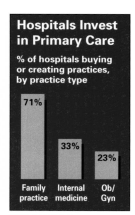

Hospitals Invest in Primary Care

% of hospitals buying or creating practices, by practice type

71% Family practice
33% Internal medicine
23% Ob/Gyn

Source: Ernst & Young

These figures, from a March 1992 survey of 315 U.S. hospitals, show that family practices are hospitals' favorite target for acquisition.

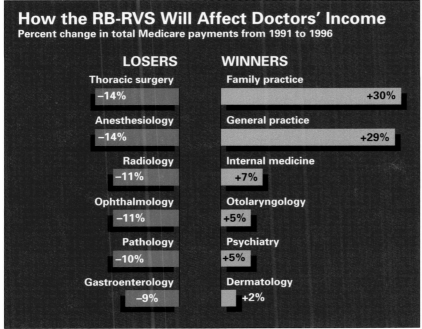

How the RB-RVS Will Affect Doctors' Income
Percent change in total Medicare payments from 1991 to 1996

LOSERS		WINNERS	
Thoracic surgery	−14%	Family practice	+30%
Anesthesiology	−14%	General practice	+29%
Radiology	−11%	Internal medicine	+7%
Ophthalmology	−11%	Otolaryngology	+5%
Pathology	−10%	Psychiatry	+5%
Gastroenterology	−9%	Dermatology	+2%

Source: Health Care Financing Administration

Medicare's resource-based relative-value scale will reduce income discrepancies between doctors. In the long run, however, changes wrought by managed care may have an even greater effect on physicians' incomes.

capitation. Such groups will have strong internal programs of utilization review, fiscal management, and information management, and the financial deep pockets to withstand the cash-flow swings of a managed-care marketplace.

And primary-care physicians' incomes are growing, while reimbursement for specialists is declining. The Kaiser Permanente Medical Group offers new family-practice residents starting salaries of up to $140,000. Improved compensation in primary care is driven by two market shifts: Medicare payment reform and managed-care capitation. Medicare's resource-based relative-value scale (RB-RVS), initiated in January 1992, is beginning to alleviate the historic imbalance in physicians' incomes (see chart, above). Blue Cross plans and other insurers are expected to adopt the RB-RVS system for physician reimbursement in the near future.

But the real money in primary care will come from capitation fees. HMOs and self-insured employers are contracting with primary-care groups to take on part or all of the financial risk for health benefits to their members. Given a continuing shortage of primary-care doctors and a surplus of specialists, it will be a sellers' market.

Real income gains for primary-care physicians will be the result, while the incomes of physicians in other specialties may stagnate. After adjusting for inflation, primary care doctors' real incomes could rise as much as 25 percent in the 1990s, with bonuses for cost-effective performance under capitated contracts. A select few primary-care physicians will be earning as much as $250,000 per year by the beginning of the 21st century .

Thus primary care will become the preferred practice of at least half of America's graduating medical students. The demand for primary-care physicians will be so strong that some medical schools will create one- or two-year specialist recycling programs to retrain subspecialists as primary-care generalists.

Many of these new doctors will enlist as gatekeepers for managed-care plans. By 2000, as many as 50 percent of all family practitioners and 25 percent of internists may be functioning as gatekeepers to control all health care utilization and costs, especially patients' access to expensive consultation or technology.

Future primary-care physicians will continue to be substantially in debt from their medical education. Many will be married. Some will already have children. A growing number will have worked in other careers before entering medical school. By 2000, well over 40 percent of young primary-care doctors will be women. These new doctors will be different. They will work for a paycheck and a pension, with reasonable working hours (50 to 55 hours per week) and limited night and weekend call. Kaiser pays overtime for more than a 40-hour week, and most Kaiser physicians work fewer than 50 hours per week.

The new doctors will be team players, care managers, gatekeepers, and front-line ethicists. Lifestyle and behavior modifications will be their major targets in patient care, and the true measure of their success will be the health of the communities they serve.

The goals of medicine are more than the absence of disease and lowered demand rates for expensive medical care. By 2000, the World Health Organization's definition of health—a state of complete physical, mental, and social well-being—will be widely accepted. This broader definition includes recognition of such health-related factors as nutrition, quality of housing, workplace safety and stress, exercise and rest, and the reduction of such health risks as smoking and consumption of alcohol and drugs.

In 2000 the primary-care physician may write a prescription for food or housing. It sounds utopian, but in hundreds of towns and cities across America, local physicians and hospitals will collaborate with social agencies and government to promote their communities' health.

Not all patients are created equal, of course. There will always be an unequal distribution of health, the result of the natural lottery (genetics) and the social lottery (environment). Not all people are winners. The most vulnerable populations include children, the elderly, the poor, the medically uninsured, the disabled, the mentally ill, the drug dependent, and the homeless.

Future primary-care physicians will be social activists as well as patient advocates. This recognition of community responsibility will widen the role of the primary physician. The new job description includes these tasks:

- Identify high-risk patients using genetics and health indicators.
- Develop personal health-improvement plans for every patient.
- Monitor the status of patients, especially those at high risk and the chronically ill.
- Take stands on public health policy issues.
- Collaborate with community organizations to address local health problems.

America is likely to fall far short of addressing its many unmet health needs. Only with concerted primary-care interventions and social activism can the U.S. hope to achieve goals like reducing infant mortality and teenage pregnancy, raising immunization levels, and increasing the functional levels of the aged and disabled.

No specialty of medicine is better positioned than primary care to improve health in America. But much must be done before primary care's new role can be realized.

The structures necessary to create the managed-care world are still being built. Doctors and hospitals in most regions of the country have yet to organize into the groups that will become the health care networks of tomorrow. As the reform juggernaut advances, however, so does the pressure on physicians to form larger and larger groups. To see what might happen soon in the nation as a whole, physicians can look at what's happening in the state of California.

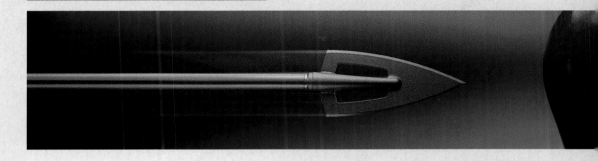

Leading the Way...

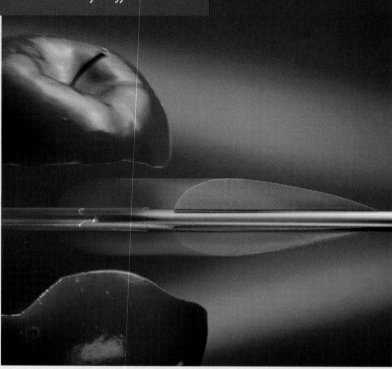

Leading the Way...
To On-target Allergy Relief

Since no two allergy sufferers are ever alike, Marion Merrell Dow provides the choices necessary for targeted relief. For treatment without drowsiness, Seldane provides impairment-free relief.[†] When nasal congestion complicates treatment, Seldane-D provides targeted congestion relief. Seldane and Seldane-D, the ideal companion products that give patients a perspective on allergy treatment that is right on target.

Because of the special considerations concerning the prescribing of Seldane and Seldane-D, please see Warnings and Contraindications sections of the prescribing information at the end of this book before prescribing these products.

Please see prescribing information at the end of this book.

[†]No more performance impairment than placebo. In clinical studies involving 300 patients, the reported incidence of drowsiness with Seldane-D (7.2%) did not differ significantly from placebo.

(terfenadine 60 mg and pseudoephedrine HCl 120 mg)
EXTENDED-RELEASE TABLETS bid

(terfenadine) 60 mg tablets
for seasonal allergic rhinitis

MARION MERRELL DOW INC.

MISAM380/B2037

0839E3

CHAPTER five

HERE COMES CALIFORNIA

Most of the building blocks for a new health-care system are emerging, even without national health reform. Want a preview? Visit California, where more than 70 percent of the non-Medicare population is enrolled in managed-care plans. California Medicare patients who are members of HMOs generate $350 to $400 per month in capitated payments, and non-Medicare patients generate $100 to $250. This represents a great deal of money, and California hospital systems are moving to consolidate with large physician groups to form regional delivery systems that contract with large managed-care buyers.

More than four million Californians are members of Kaiser Permanente, the nation's largest and oldest HMO. Kaiser's system demonstrates how cost-effective this type of managed care can be. Extrapolating from its pattern of physician use, if every American were enrolled in a similar plan, the U.S. would need only 363,000 doctors, as opposed to the 600,000 doctors licensed in 1993. One reason: Kaiser Permanente's hospital-use rates are Spartan. In Northern California, Kaiser averaged only 361 hospital inpatient days per 1,000 members in 1991, compared with 887 for the nation as a whole. A look at Kaiser's Northern California 1991 utilization patterns for five common procedures shows how its system could provide substantial savings if implemented everywhere:

• Hysterectomy. Kaiser has a discharge rate of 142 per 100,000 enrollees, compared with 238 per 100,000 for the U.S. as a whole. The potential cost savings if Kaiser's pattern were adopted throughout the country: $1.2 billion.

• Laminectomy. Kaiser's discharge rate is 38 per 100,000, compared with 122 per 100,000 for the U.S. The potential savings: $1 billion.

• Cholecystectomy. Kaiser has 129 discharges per 100,000 enrollees, compared with a nationwide rate of 209. The potential savings: $989 million.

• Angioplasty. Kaiser's rate of 38 per 100,000 compares with a U.S. rate of 114. The potential savings: $940 million.

• CABG. Kaiser's rate is 67 per 100,000, compared with a nationwide rate of 106. The potential savings: $482 million.

Other California providers and managed-care plans are scrambling to create health-care organizations that can compete with Kaiser. In June 1993 California Blue Shield and UniHealth America, an 11-hospital system based in Los Angeles, announced plans to explore a merger that would create a statewide health organization with more than three million subscribers, second only to Kaiser. UniHealth has also created a medical subsidiary, UniMed America, which will acquire the assets of large physician practices and consolidate them into nonprofit medical-clinic foundations. (One reason medical foundations are so popular in California is that their organizational structure allows health care systems to avoid violating the state's ban on the corporate practice of medicine.)

Also in 1993, the 601-bed Loma Linda University Medical Center, together with the 160-physician Friendly Hills Medical Group of La Habra, California, created a medical foundation in a $125 million deal that included a doctor-owned 160-bed hospital. The Internal Revenue Service approved nonprofit status for the foundation, clearing the way to pay for the transaction with an $80 million bond offering to supplement the hospital's $30 million and a $15 million loan from the physicians.

In Sacramento, Sutter Health, a nonprofit system with 14 acute-care hospitals, 2,400 physicians, four skilled-nursing facilities, and two HMOs, affiliated with the 126-doctor Sacramento-Sierra Medical Group, an innovative group practice without walls, in 1992. Since then, Sutter Health has affiliated with five other physician groups, the largest of which is the 160-doctor, multispecialty Palo Alto Medical Foundation.

The increase in market share from creating such organizations can be substantial. In 1985 the Sharp HealthCare system of San Diego acquired the Rees-Stealy Medical Group, a multispecialty group practice that has since grown to 275 physicians. In 1992 Sharp bought the 88-physician Mission Park Medical Clinic of Vista, California, and recently it strengthened its physician network by affiliating with the Sharp Community Medical Group, a 435-doctor independent-practice association with 135 primary-care physicians and more than 300 specialists. Thus Sharp HealthCare, with five hospitals totaling 1,291 beds, seven physician group practices, 14 clinics, and four skilled-nursing facilities, is emerging as one of three dominant health systems in the San Diego area. Its 325,000 enrollees under 60 to 70 managed-care contracts, more than 20 of which are capitated, represent 25 percent of the market.

A key factor in Sharp's success in this heavily managed-care marketplace is its partnership with seven primary-care physician groups, all of which hold risk-sharing, capitated contracts. The Sharp system as a whole has pluralistic relationships with the rest of its physicians. Some are employed by group practices or are members of IPAs, and others are independent members of the various hospitals' medical staffs.

The Sharp system has devised various methods to control costs. It will devote $30 million to develop and install by 1996 a regional information system that will centralize financial and clinical data in a single electronic medical record. To further reduce costs, the company is collaborating with physicians to develop practice guidelines and clinical protocols.

It's not just hospitals and health systems that are getting into the act. Physicians can organize their own structures. In the vanguard of physicians' response to the managed-care takeover is the Mullikin Medical Group of Artesia, California, a 400-doctor multisite, multispecialty group practice that has 22 HMO contracts covering 300,000 enrollees. Mullikin is the medical-group market leader in the dynamic managed-care arena of Southern California, and it plans to expand into Northern California by forging statewide partnerships with HMOs and hospital systems. Recently, the six-hospital Daughters of Charity Health System-West Region in San Francisco made a multimillion-dollar investment in Mullikin, allowing the medical group to solidify strategic alliances with the three Daughters of Charity hospitals in Los Angeles and other compatible institutions in the system. In Northern California Mullikin has acquired a 250-doctor medical group, positioning itself to support the three Daughters of Charity facilities in the Bay Area.

Mullikin believes physicians should be owners as well as employees: some 200 of the group's 400 physicians hold equity shares. Physician compensation is non-production-based (that is, it's not tied to how many patients a doctor sees in a day), with salary levels pegged at the 75th percentile of the Medical Group Management Association (MGMA) statistics for comparable specialties. Doctors are compensated for the time they spend on management. And since physician owners receive a return on their equity, they have an incentive to work for group goals.

As a result, Mullikin's utilization patterns are startlingly low. The group holds inpatient days to 180 per 1,000 enrollees under age 65, compared with a national average of about 600. Mullikin's Medicare bed days run about 1,000 per 1,000 Medicare HMO enrollees. Other medical groups, including California Primary Physicians and the Friendly Hills Medical Group, have even tighter ratios, in the range of 750 to 800 days per 1,000 Medicare participants.

Mullikin will contract with preferred-provider organizations only if they also have an HMO; the group will then seek to persuade the PPO enrollees to join the HMO alternative. Hospitals that affiliate are paid by capitation, sharing the risks and the rewards. They must agree to place restraints on their radiologists, anesthesiologists, and pathologists, because per diem payments only encourage longer stays. Mullikin's hospital partners have experienced a

A Shift in Perspective…

At Marion Merrell Dow
We Do It Right the First Time…

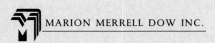

decline in the share of their business devoted to acute inpatient care, but they can make up the lost revenues by expanding into nonacute continuing care and ambulatory-care services. Mental health is incorporated as part of primary care, and health promotion is strongly emphasized.

California groups like Kaiser, Mullikin, Sharp, and UniHealth America are responding to market pressures on employers that began to be felt in the state in the mid- to late '80s, when businesses found profits threatened by ever-increasing costs for employees' health insurance. As a result, companies began to experiment with direct-contracting agreements for health care.

The best-known of these arrangements is the one created by Southern California Edison (SCE), a utility whose health costs quadrupled from $21 million to $82 million between 1981 and 1988, an average of 22 percent per year. In 1988 the company found itself facing a requested premium increase of 27 percent for the next year. So Edison decided to design and manage its own health system for its 55,000 employees, dependents, and retirees.

The company brought in Dr. Jacques Sokolov, a medical consultant, as vice-president and medical director of its new self-funded and internally administered health care plan. Sokolov's department created from scratch its own preferred-provider network of 85 hospitals, 7,500 physicians, and eight company-owned primary-care medical clinics, and it translated Edison's market clout into better discounts from providers than the company's former insurance plan had been able to negotiate. SCE's health-care department is now administrator, insurer, and provider of services to all 55,000 of Edison's plan participants in Southern California.

The strategy that Sokolov and SCE developed to control health costs relies on five components:

• Managed-care contracts with a network of preferred providers and a program of utilization management and quality assurance. (Utilization management focuses on catastrophic care, psychiatric treatment, drug and alcohol treatment, and outpatient surgery.)

• The direct operation of a company-owned network of eight

primary-care centers, which provide less expensive care than community physicians do.

• Pricing the company's managed-indemnity plan so attractively that few employees or retirees will choose any of the other three HMOs available to them over the company plan.

• Encouraging preventive health care by offering a Good Health Rebate of $10 per month to employees who complete an annual screening for modifiable risk factors such as smoking, hypertension, and hypercholesteremia. Employees also receive $100 a year each to pay for such preventive health measures as smoking-cessation classes and elective mammography.

• Restructuring the retirement plan so that retirees are given the option of receiving 100 percent coverage from the company's preferred-provider network or 80 percent coverage if they choose care outside the network.

As a consequence of these measures, Edison's savings are substantial. Assuming conservatively that its costs would have risen 18 percent each year (as have health expenditures at other large companies), Edison saved $28 million in the first two years of the program. The company's health-cost inflation slowed to 9 percent a year between 1988, when the plan was started, and 1992, when total costs were $114 million. Edison's savings from 1989 through 1992 are estimated at $66 million. In 1993 SCE was negotiating with its original insurer, Aetna, to become network manager.

Edison's plan, a cost-effective integrated health system with primary care at its heart and a strong emphasis on prevention, is a model for self-insured employers. Other large companies have asked to buy in. If Edison does so, it will further increase its buyer's clout and create new opportunities for system efficiency.

Other big buyers are catching on. CalPERS, California's Public Employees Retirement System, contracts with HMOs statewide to take care of its nearly 900,000 workers, retirees, and dependents. The size of this pool gives CalPERS enormous buyer's clout. Contracting with 19 HMOs and seven insurance plans, it managed to hold its health premium inflation to only 1.5 percent in 1993, compared with a national average of 14 to 18 percent, because HMOs agreed to forfeit cost increases to keep CalPERS enrollees.

"CalPERS doesn't pay list price for health care anymore," said benefits administrator Tom Elkin at a February 1993 press conference. "By demanding cost and performance data, we have become a better-informed consumer. Now we can do some comparison shopping before we write the check."

One of CalPERS' advisers is Alain Enthoven, the creator of managed competition. Not long after the February press conference, health care industry journalists began to write that CalPERS' success in bargaining with its providers not only represented the first real-life test of Enthoven's theory, but its first victory. CalPERS critics say that the test was meaningless because California's marketplace is still unregulated enough to allow HMOs that give discounts to one group to shift the cost to others who will pay more. Even Enthoven has his doubts. True managed competition, the economist told the *Los Angeles Times*, would require CalPERS to create incentives for the enrollees themselves to save money. Taxing benefits that exceeded those offered in the basic package might be one way to do that, Enthoven said. But whether the CalPERS system is managed competition in action or merely a powerful buying group, others are trying to imitate its success: two more buying cooperatives, one to consolidate buying for small businesses and another an alliance of large businesses in the San Francisco area, are being developed.

Another successful approach to lowering employer health care costs is found at the California company AlliedSignal, which has been contracting with Cigna since 1988 to provide managed care for its 110,000 workers, dependents, and retirees. Cigna organized 29 physician-hospital networks in cities where AlliedSignal has local operations. AlliedSignal workers who sign up for the managed-care plan are not required to see plan physicians exclusively, but they must pay an extra 20 percent of the bill if they use physicians outside the network. The company has cut its health care inflation in half, to less than 9 percent per year, compared with 18 percent for traditional indemnity plans. AlliedSignal's employees are satisfied, too. An independent survey found that 85 percent like their care, a rate that's only slightly lower than for people with traditional insurance.

As a result of these successes, major employers like the Bank of America, Wells Fargo & Company, and the state of California are choosing regional or statewide plans over smaller HMOs and PPOs. Wells Fargo has reportedly reduced the choice of health plans it offers employees to two HMOs, Kaiser and Health Net.

Not all of the companies that are taking direct responsibility for employees' health care are in California. The John Deere Corporation of Moline, Illinois, has provided managed health care to its employees since 1980, when the company created its own HMO in the Moline area and contracted for capitated care with various independent practice associations. The effort was so successful that Deere went on to create John Deere Health Care and an operating company, Heritage National Healthplan, to offer managed-care services to other employers. Deere now has over 300 clients, including Eastman Kodak and Monsanto Chemical Company.

Deere is moving to integrate its HMO system more closely with the provider community through a strategic alliance with the Mayo Clinic of Rochester, Minnesota. In 1991 John Deere Health Care announced that Mayo would collaborate in the design, setup, and administration of the first John Deere Family Health Center. The center, which would be staffed with eight primary-care doctors, would provide front-line care for employees and dependents and retirees in the Moline area under a new HMO: the John Deere Family Health Plan. The center opened in January 1993, and Mayo continues to work with Deere staff physicians to develop practice guidelines and quality and utilization management systems. A Mayo employee is administrator for the Deere center.

Workers who choose the Deere-Mayo option have no out-of-pocket health care costs. Although the option was negotiated in 1991 with the United Auto Workers, it is open to all Deere employees, and the company reports that 4,000 employees signed up in the first six months that the plan was offered. Analysts expect savings of 15 to 30 percent because Deere uses a staff-model approach and strict patient management. Eventually Deere hopes to attract about 15,000 participants, a prospect that will dismay local IPA physicians who fear losing patients.

Again cooperating with Mayo, Deere announced plans to open a second family care clinic near Waterloo, Iowa, in 1994, and to invite other local companies to participate. Mayo will consult with Deere to develop model practice guidelines, and the clinic will be the preferred supplier of specialty services to Deere health plan enrollees. This strategic alliance between Deere and Mayo is a good example of how physician groups can contract directly with employers—as long as employers are committed to quality as well as cost control and active participation in the plan's administration.

What other lessons do these experiments offer physicians, hospitals, and major employers? First, health costs are not uncontrollable. There is enough money in the current system, if it is well managed, to provide good primary and specialty health coverage for all. Second, the buyer's involvement in health-cost management can be highly rewarding. Third, in a period of public debate over national health reform, these innovative experiments demonstrate that local reform efforts based on collaboration between purchasers and providers can restrain health costs. Finally, it seems almost inevitable that what has been accomplished in California will soon be imitated throughout the United States.

CHAPTER six

PHYSICIAN- HOSPITAL ORGANIZATIONS

T he forces that propelled the consolidation of physicians, hospitals, and health plans in California—the enroll- ment of large groups of patients in managed-care plans and pressure from both employers and government to lower the cost of medical care while increasing access to the system—are now at large in the nation as a whole. Very soon successful physician groups will have to demonstrate not only their ability to survive under capitation but their ability to keep patients healthy. In most parts of the U.S., however, unlike California, physicians and hos- pitals are not organized to practice in such a system.

Many medical practices lack the organizational discipline and commitment necessary to succeed in managed care, says Steve McDermott, CEO of the Hill Physicians' Medical Group in San Ramon, California. Because they are financially and structurally unsound, such practices are seriously vulnerable. In the San Fran- cisco Bay area, for example, McDermott notes that seven medical groups have filed for bankruptcy in the past four years. The groups' inability to handle managed-care contracting played a role in all seven cases.

John McDonald, CEO of the Mullikin Medical Group, believes many physician groups are too democratic: weak governance structures (one doctor, one board seat) diminish their ability to make business decisions that benefit the organization rather than the individual doctors. Such groups may have inadequate financial reserves, for example, because they don't retain earnings. This limits their ability to upgrade facilities, expand sites, or take risk-based contracts. Other groups have not yet upgraded to accrual-based accounting systems, or they have poor management-information systems that hobble the doctors' ability to manage care or costs. Or they may use production-based compensation, which reduces the synergy of group practice. Physicians in groups should work collaboratively to share capitation and performance incentives, says McDonald.

Hospitals are similarly unprepared. The traditional hospital medical staff is set up to credential members and manage quality. It is not structured to manage costs or to contract on behalf of physicians for managed-care patients. But as managed care and national health reform push physicians and hospitals together, health care provider organizations will be converted from revenue to cost centers. Ultimately such organizations will save money by reducing use through supply-side management and reducing demand through measures aimed at disease prevention and health promotion.

This calls for a fundamental reorganization of the relationship between physicians and hospitals. To make the transition, doctors and hospitals will need a new model of collaborative management. The key elements of this new model:

• The ability to manage patients under capitation contracts that involve the sharing of risks.

• The development of a comprehensive service package that can be offered by a vertically organized health system.

• The organization of primary-care and specialty physicians into a metropolitan or regional network.

• A systemwide set of standards of care and clinical protocols to manage high-cost procedures and high-volume diagnoses.

• Aggressive management of clinical costs and utilization.

• An information base and computer network to monitor decision making and outcomes.

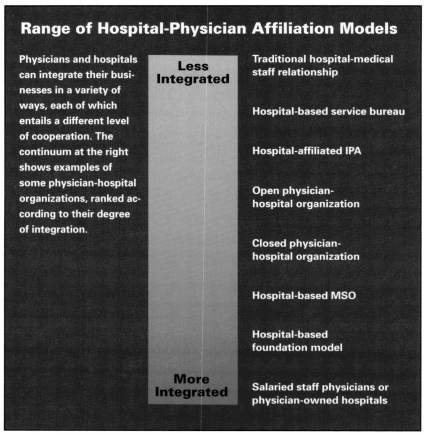

Range of Hospital-Physician Affiliation Models

Physicians and hospitals can integrate their businesses in a variety of ways, each of which entails a different level of cooperation. The continuum at the right shows examples of some physician-hospital organizations, ranked according to their degree of integration.

Less Integrated

More Integrated

Traditional hospital-medical staff relationship

Hospital-based service bureau

Hospital-affiliated IPA

Open physician-hospital organization

Closed physician-hospital organization

Hospital-based MSO

Hospital-based foundation model

Salaried staff physicians or physician-owned hospitals

Source: The Health Forecasting Group

• Hiring medical executives to manage medical group practices and physician networks.

Physicians and hospitals can use a range of organizational options to create such models, options that allow progressively closer relationships, from cooperation to integration (see chart, above). Loosely speaking, any alliances between physicians and hospitals are called physician-hospital organizations (PHOs). Although PHOs are a transitional mechanism in the development of integrated health systems, they may be the most important building block for constructing government-approved health plans of doctors, hospitals, and insurers under national health reform.

The primary purpose of a PHO is to enable physicians and hospitals to contract jointly with buyers of managed care. But there

A Shift in Perspective...

Repair and Maintenance

Repair and Maintenance With Carafate

Even a classic work of art such as the Sistine Chapel ceiling requires repair in order to ensure the maintenance of its natural beauty. For the duodenal ulcer patient, CARAFATE works directly at the ulcer site to protect from further attack by acid, pepsin, and bile salts. And CARAFATE can also help maintain healed duodenal ulcers in remission. Nonsystemic ulcer therapy that protects locally, accelerates healing, and maintains remission...that's repair and maintenance with CARAFATE.

Please see prescribing information at the end of this book.

CARAFATE®
(sucralfate) 1gm tablets

MARION MERRELL DOW INC.

are other reasons physicians might benefit from such an arrangement. The most important is that hospitals have capital reserves. Money in the bank not only helps buffer the risk-sharing features of managed-care contracts; it can also be used to expand the physician group, to purchase other groups, to provide recruitment incentives and practice guarantees for new members, and to cash out retiring members. Moreover, a unified organization can provide centralized management-information systems, utilization review, and quality assurance.

Despite these advantages, many physicians remain confused about PHOs. Does affiliation mean that the hospital owns the physician's practice? Does it mean that physicians are put on salary? It can mean either, but basically a PHO creates a partnership between equals. The corporate structure is usually a 50-50 joint venture between doctors and a hospital or health system. Physicians may be organized into an independent practice association that contracts with the PHO, or they may simply be shareholders in the PHO. The PHO may be nonprofit or for-profit. It may include every doctor on a hospital's medical staff, or just one medical group practice. Hospitals may have more than one PHO for different purposes, such as direct contracting with a local employer, and physicians may belong to more than one PHO.

There are six basic models, three that are familiar to almost every U.S. physician and three that are not as well known. They are the independent-practice association, the preferred-provider organization, the health-maintenance organization, the direct-contracting joint venture, the management-service organization (MSO), and the foundation.

The independent-practice association. An IPA is an easily created, low-cost mechanism that gives independent physicians a way to contract jointly with insurance plans and managed-care buyers. One of the earliest models for organizing physicians, the IPA simply creates an umbrella organization that allows independent doctors to accept managed-care contracts that the IPA negotiates. IPAs may be sponsored by hospitals or medical societies, and physicians are typically paid on a discounted fee-for-service basis. Most are not organized to take risk-sharing capitation contracts, but during the next three years, many will restructure so they can do so. In a number of hospitals and health systems, this may create two IPAs; the original one, with the larger, more inclusive physician membership, will take only fee-for-service contracts, whereas the smaller one will consist of physicians willing and organized to take the risk of capitation.

IPAs offer a useful way for specialists to organize so they can accept capitation and subcapitation. The specialty IPA is often affiliated with a hospital, but entrepreneurial physicians in some markets have successfully established freestanding IPAs .

The preferred-provider organization. The PPO is a non-risk-sharing venture that channels patients to selected physicians and hospitals that have agreed to accept discounted payments. Begun in the mid-1970s, PPOs come in numerous variations, but basically they are used to avoid antitrust limitations on providers' price-setting. Existing PPOs pay doctors on a discounted fee-for-service basis, but in the future, they will restructure like HMOs to take capitation contracts.

The health-maintenance organization. After the economic failure of a number of HMOs in the 1970s and '80s, many hospitals and health systems decided against owning HMOs. But the concept is enjoying a renaissance. In 1992, according to a *Modern Healthcare* survey, the revenues of hospital-owned HMO plans rose to $2.9 billion, a 12 percent increase over 1991 and a 170 percent jump from 1988. Provider-owned plans, thanks to a 15 percent boost in enrollment in 1992, averaged almost $2 million in net income, up 20 percent from 1991. Five provider-owned HMOs—led by Henry Ford's Health Alliance Plan of Michigan, with a $12.9 million surplus on revenues of $630.5 million—made more than $5 million in 1992. The number of these provider-sponsored HMOs is likely to double in the next five years as hospitals and doctors begin to build integrated health systems that can become certified health plans or regional delivery networks.

HMO physicians may be paid on a discounted fee-for-service basis or by sharing capitation. Primary-care physicians are often capitated. The *InterStudy Edge* reported in 1992 that HMOs used various methods to pay primary-care physicians, including capitation (72.4 percent), discounted fee-for-service (42.3 percent), negotiated fee schedule (33 percent), fee-for-service (23.5 percent), relative value scale (15.8 percent), salary (13.6 percent), and others (9.5 percent).

The direct-contracting venture. This model is an option for hospitals that seek to avoid the regulations and reserve requirements of HMOs. In such deals, hospitals and physician groups take direct economic risk for capitation contracts, cutting out the middleman (i.e., the insurance company or the government). The Mayo Clinic's contract to provide specialty and subspecialty care to John Deere Health Plan enrollees is a good example of such an arrangement. Like HMOs, direct-contracting plans may reimburse physicians in a variety of ways. If doctors and hospitals engage in direct contracting as a joint venture, physicians can specify their preferred mode of payment. But because direct contracting puts hospitals and doctors at financial risk, many of these arrangements put physicians under capitation to limit medical expenditures. In 1992 Michigan's Medicaid program, while not abandoning fee-for-service, switched emphasis to managed care so that it could contract directly with HMOs and PHOs to capitate more than one million Medicaid enrollees across the state.

The management-service organization. MSOs can be used to integrate physicians with hospitals in a variety of ways, from a very loose partnership to a completely integrated one. They may contract with individual physician practices and medical groups to provide administrative services such as billing and claims; to integrate managed-care contracting into a single entity; to provide support services such as information systems, personnel, human resources, group purchasing, and benefits management; to buy the hard assets of physician practices; to manage physician practices; or to acquire all of a practice's assets. MSOs are useful in states that have laws forbidding the corporate practice of medicine, because they provide services only to the physicians in the contracting group, not to patients.

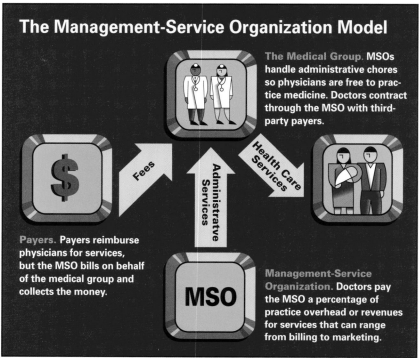

The Management-Service Organization Model

The Medical Group. MSOs handle administrative chores so physicians are free to practice medicine. Doctors contract through the MSO with third-party payers.

Fees

Administrative Services

Health Care Services

$

Payers. Payers reimburse physicians for services, but the MSO bills on behalf of the medical group and collects the money.

MSO

Management-Service Organization. Doctors pay the MSO a percentage of practice overhead or revenues for services that can range from billing to marketing.

Source: The Health Forecasting Group

Physicians can affiliate with MSOs—which may be freestanding or hospital-affiliated—in a variety of ways. In all cases, doctors receive administrative services in exchange for a percentage of practice overhead or revenues.

Management-service organizations may be freestanding or hospital-affiliated. The freestanding MSO is an independent, taxable business corporation that may be owned by lay investors or physicians, and this type of business is becoming increasingly popular. For example, many doctors are being approached by Nashville-based PhyCor, a five-year-old company whose revenues have grown from $63.9 million in 1990 to an estimated $180 million in 1993. PhyCor, which buys and manages physician practices, owns clinics in nine states and has 500 physician affiliates.

Whether freestanding or hospital affiliated, MSOs furnish facilities, equipment and supplies, staff, and administrative services to physician corporations under turnkey management-services agreements that define the terms of service and responsibilities between

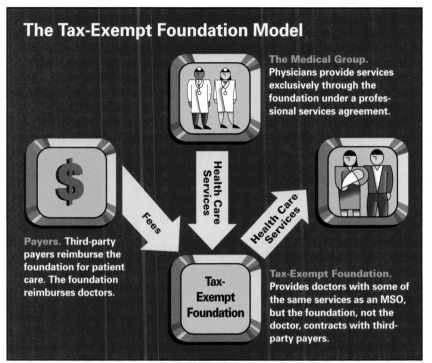

The Tax-Exempt Foundation Model

The Medical Group. Physicians provide services exclusively through the foundation under a professional services agreement.

Health Care Services

Payers. Third-party payers reimburse the foundation for patient care. The foundation reimburses doctors.

Fees

Health Care Services

Tax-Exempt Foundation

Tax-Exempt Foundation. Provides doctors with some of the same services as an MSO, but the foundation, not the doctor, contracts with third-party payers.

Source: The Health Forecasting Group

The foundation model provides doctors with some of the same administrative services as the MSO, but because the foundation owns the managed-care contracts, physicians have less control over their patient base.

the parties. The MSO bills on behalf of the physician group and may also manage other groups and entities. The medical professional corporation employs primary-care or multispecialty physicians to provide services to patients and payers, and may have a single owner (a physician) or multiple owners (several physicians or entrepreneurs). The physicians own and operate all the medical aspects of the group practice and they also "own" the charts and patients.

A hospital-affiliated MSO also contracts with a group of physicians, but it may be separately incorporated or operated as a division of a hospital or health system. Unlike the freestanding MSO, which is a taxable business corporation, it may qualify for 501(c)(3) tax-exempt status. Like the freestanding model, the hospital-affiliated MSO provides the physician group with all facilities, equipment and supplies, staff, and support services. The MSO contracts with third-party payers, bills for the physicians, and may manage other groups and entities. The doctors' group is a physician-owned professional corporation, composed of either primary or multi-specialty doctors. It provides services to patients and may be affiliated with an independent-practice association. The physician corporation owns and operates the clinical aspects of the group practice, owns the charts, patients, and managed-care contracts and employs individual physicians. Because this is a form of physician-hospital partnership, physicians can specify their preferred mode of payment.

Capital, which may come from a hospital, an HMO, or an entrepreneur, is a major factor when medical groups decide whether or not to affiliate with an MSO. Affiliation strengthens the group for recruitment, growth, managed-care contracting, and other strategic objectives. A hospital or health system can offer management expertise and administrative support services, helping the group practice to achieve such goals as professional collegiality and economic stability and security. Relieved of the business, financial, and administrative hassles of managing a group practice, physicians are at liberty to practice medicine.

The foundation. The tax-exempt, nonprofit medical foundation can be organized as a freestanding center, as an affiliate of a hospital through a common parent organization, or as a wholly owned subsidiary of a hospital. Like MSOs, foundation models circumvent laws against the corporate practice of medicine; unlike MSOs, foundations can provide care directly to patients. The freestanding medical foundation is a tax-exempt 501(c)(3) organization that often has a strong research and education purpose. The Mayo and Cleveland clinics are perhaps the best-known medical foundations in the county. Foundations may be owned by a hospital or health system, or by a freestanding medical group practice.

A tax-exempt clinic may affiliate with a hospital or health system for managed-care contracting or other shared purposes—to provide a primary-care base or operate an ambulatory-care center, for example. Or a hospital may own the medical foundation outright, which gives the hospital greater control of the group practices that contract with the foundation through professional services agreements. Whether freestanding, affiliated, or wholly owned, all medical-foundation models operate group practices, own the practice sites, facilities, and equipment, employ all nonphysician staff members, contract with patients and payers in managed-care arrangements, and bill under a common provider number.

Foundations contract for medical services with a professional corporation that is wholly owned by physicians. The medical group practice may offer primary or multispecialty care. The physician corporation employs the doctors and provides medical services to the foundation under a professional-services agreement. In most such arrangements, the medical foundation holds a significant amount of the capital assets (land, facilities, equipment, financial reserves), and the professional corporation has relatively few capital assets. Medical clinic foundations are likely to use salaries as the predominant method of paying physicians. Teaching and research are often integral parts of patient care.

No matter what kind of affiliation physicians and hospitals decide to pursue, they must begin by disclosing their present managed-care statuses and concerns. Allan Fine, vice-president and director of the Center for Managed Care of Quorum Health Resources in Chicago, advises doctors to put their cards on the table, revealing which managed-care plans they currently contract with, which plans are most important to them, and which they'd like to add. The hospital must be equally open about the managed-care contracts it holds, revealing to physicians which are profitable and which break even or lose money. Then doctors and hospital representatives should have a frank discussion of how to better integrate their managed-care activities so as to increase mutual leverage with HMOs, managed-care organizations, and insurers. The litmus test of how well the process is working, suggests Fine, is a mutual decision not to contract with a particular managed-care plan because it would benefit only one side.

Once a formal decision to pursue integration is made, physicians should be involved from the start, with full and equal representation on the organizing committee and the resulting PHO board. Doctors should rotate with hospital representatives to chair the new board, and all study groups should have equal participation. Every important PHO committee should have equal physician participation, and physicians should chair many committees. All major medical specialties should be involved in the PHO formation discussions, but solo specialists shouldn't be surprised if the hospital gives higher status to large group practices, especially primary-care groups. Most PHOs will need to be heavily staffed by primary-care doctors because they are so critical to future success under managed care.

Both physicians and the hospital or health system should contribute to the initial capitalization of the PHO, even if doctors are only willing or able to contribute symbolic amounts in the development phase (this is an area for legal advice, to avoid running afoul of rules governing Medicare and Medicaid). To expedite the formation process, the hospital may loan capital to the PHO, with a long-term or deferred payback program. Within three to five years, or once the PHO has contracts for 25,000 to 40,000 enrollees, it should be able to repay the initial capitalization.

How much does it cost to start a PHO? John Marren, formerly an attorney with Katten, Muchin & Zavis in Chicago, estimates start-up expenses at $100,000 or more, with annual operating costs of $150,000 to $1.5 million. In a recent interview in the *Medical Staff Strategy Report*, Marren estimated that two-thirds of a hospital's active medical staff will join a PHO. Most PHOs will not be money-makers, but their primary value is the creation of a mechanism by which physicians and hospitals can jointly contract with managed-care buyers.

As physicians and hospitals move into consolidated arrangements, antitrust laws will be an issue. The American Hospital Association is concerned that aggressive enforcement of the Sherman Antitrust Act could hamper efforts to develop the regional health networks that national health reform will require. Government

Clearing the air...

Clearing the air
changes your
outlook on life

Nicotine addiction can be like living in a haze. Withdrawal symptoms are difficult to overcome. Marion Merrell Dow, a leader in smoking cessation, can lessen the severity of nicotine withdrawal symptoms for your patients who attempt to quit smoking. NICODERM® (nicotine transdermal system) is a 10-week regimen of controlled nicotine dosing in a transdermal nicotine patch. In a hazy world, NICODERM helps begin the shift in perspective to a healthy, smoke-free life.

NICODERM is indicated as an aid to smoking cessation for the relief of nicotine withdrawal symptoms. NICODERM should be used as part of a comprehensive behavioral smoking-cessation program. The use of NICODERM for longer than 3 months has not been studied. Patients should be instructed to stop smoking immediately and not use any other nicotine-containing products during treatment. The specific effects of NICODERM on fetal development are unknown. Therefore, pregnant or nursing smokers should be encouraged to attempt cessation using educational and behavioral interventions before using pharmacological approaches. The risks of nicotine replacement in patients with certain cardiovascular and peripheral vascular diseases should be weighed against the benefits of including nicotine replacement in a smoking-cessation program for them. Dosage adjustment of concomitant medications may be necessary. (See Drug Interactions.)

Please see prescribing information at the end of this book.

NICODERM®
[nicotine transdermal system]

MARION MERRELL DOW INC.

agencies argue that they have challenged only five mergers from some 200 hospital consolidations in the past five years, but many hospitals have been reluctant to pursue consolidation discussions because of antitrust concerns. Physicians should share this concern: doctors' efforts to set prices for HMO contracting have been challenged successfully as price-fixing and a violation of the Sherman Act.

Generally the Federal Trade Commission and the Justice Department become concerned about possible restraint of trade when an organization captures 20 percent of the potential market. (Ventures that exceed the limit may still pass muster under specific circumstances defined by the FTC.) But national health reformers envision consumers selecting from a limited number of local health care networks. How many networks can there be? The Clinton health care task force assumes there would be at least six choices in each market. Realistically, only three or four provider networks can compete except in the largest metropolitan areas, and only one or two will exist in lightly populated areas. And even though there may be multiple insurance plans as HMOs and self-funded employers provide consumer choices, such plans will be forced to contract with a limited number of systems. Unless the antitrust problem is recognized by Congress, the goal of cost-efficient competing systems may never be realized.

Some hospitals are already moving aggressively to link with other hospitals and physicians and capture a dominant market position just under the antitrust threshold. The do-it-now strategy of network development is intended to preempt competitors and tie up the most desired facilities, locations, and doctors. Antitrust attorneys can help keep these networking activities within generally accepted limits by identifying any problem that might raise red flags at the Federal Trade Commission or the Justice Department.

What can physicians do at the local level? Here are 10 strategies to pursue:

• Assess your environment and your capacities. Gain an in-depth understanding of the changes occurring in your medical marketplace. Understand the dynamics of change as it will affect others, including other physicians, medical groups, hospitals, health plans, employers, and the government. Make a realistic appraisal of your strengths and weaknesses as a participant in the changing medical environment.

• Think about what competitors will do. Talk with other physicians and health care organizations in your community. Discuss their strategies for responding to the changes ahead; most will speak candidly. The elements of community health systems are being organized now. Forecast what the major players will do and figure out where you and your practice fit in.

• Identify potential partners. Under health reform and managed care, the future health care marketplace will create contracts with regional networks of medical organizations and hospitals. Talk with potential partners. Seek an alignment of your values with their vision of a future system. Partnerships are about values, not economics. Look for relationships that engender a feeling of trust.

• Develop a five-year plan. Your future should happen by design, not chance. Make a long-range business and development plan for yourself and your practice. Set short-term and five-year goals, then identify how you will achieve your preferred future. Invest in systems and strategies that further your practice goals.

• Build a group practice. The market wants medical groups. Ally with other physicians and build a single-specialty, multispecialty, or network-model group to contract with managed-care plans. Choose like-minded physicians who also value quality and efficiency. Bring on professional management and delegate leadership to a small "corporate" board that can manage the group like a business.

• Calculate your costs of care. Know your costs for providing every routine and specialized procedure, for in-office procedures and hospitalized patients. Look at variations in your costs, and compare your charges with those of your peers using available community or national databases.

• Install a quality-monitoring system. Physicians will ultimately be judged on the quality of their clinical outcomes as well as customer satisfaction levels. Purchase and use quality-monitoring systems or participate in local systems available from community hospitals.

• Manage your costs and utilization patterns. Be a cost-efficient provider before the market demands it. Develop the discipline of managing every patient for the lowest cost while maintaining quality. Prepare treatment protocols and critical paths for managing your most frequent diagnoses and procedures.

• Engage in risk-sharing capitation contracts. Take capitation contracts as early as possible. Physicians open to risk-sharing arrangements will be preferred by managed-care plans and self-insured employers. Physicians who cling to fee-for-service arrangements will miss this window of opportunity. Managed-care buyers may knock on a doctor's door only once.

• Commit to a hospital or system and selected health plans. The time for partnership is here. Identify preferred partners and make long-term commitments. Invest with hospitals and health plans in building community-wide systems. The independent practice of medicine is ending. Only organized health systems will have the staying power under national reform and managed care. Choose your system now and build for a shared future.

All-payer system. A health care financing plan that assigns uniform fees for all medical services, regardless of who pays for the service.

Capitation. A reimbursement method that pays a set fee per patient per month in exchange for all medical care. This type of approach puts physicians and hospitals at financial risk. In some systems, primary-care physicians may manage the capitation fee, setting aside a portion of it to pay specialists and hospitals. This process is called subcapitation.

Clinic without walls. A group practice that operates from multiple sites. Member practices are usually economically linked and share a common administration.

Continuous quality improvement (CQI). A quality-control system that many hospitals use to continuously monitor the treatment a patient receives. Some hospitals using CQI have reduced the average length of stay while maintaining patient satisfaction. (Also called total quality management, or TQM.)

Covered lives. In capitated systems, the total patient base.

Direct-contracting venture. A health plan—often sponsored by a self-insured employer—that buys care directly from physicians, rather than through an intermediary. Direct contracting is often used as a model in open panel HMOs (see *HMO*).

Discounted fee-for-service. A reimbursement system commonly used by preferred-provider plans in which physicians agree to provide care to a health plan's patients at a discount from the customary fee. The discount may be further reduced by a "withhold," a sum that the payer deducts from the initial payment and withholds until the end of the year, when it is reimbursed to physicians only if they meet cost-saving goals.

Economic credentialing. Hard data about an individual physician's performance collected to measure the doctor's cost efficiency. Hospitals may use economic credentialing to decide which physicians to add to (or drop from) their staffs. Managed-care plans credential physicians for the same reason.

Gatekeeper. A physician, most commonly a primary-care specialist, who supervises all aspects of a patient's care and who must authorize care from all other providers (except in emergencies) before it can be rendered. This is a common feature of HMOs.

Health-insurance purchasing corporation (HIPC). An entity that acts as a health-insurance purchasing agent for large groups of people. HIPCs are an important feature of managed competition.

Health-maintenance organization (HMO). A prepaid health plan in which doctors are paid a fixed fee to treat patients covered by the plan (see *capitation*). HMOs may employ physicians as salaried staff members or they may contract with a specific physician group (a closed panel) or with any physician in a community who can accept capitation (an open panel).

Independent-practice association (IPA). A legal entity that holds managed-care contracts. The IPA contracts with physicians to provide care on a fee-for-service or capitation basis. IPAs are often sponsored by medical societies to help physicians in solo practice contract for managed care.

Managed care. The meaning of this phrase is still evolving, but generally it refers to a method of delivering, supervising, and coordinating health care so as to control costs and maintain quality. The system works in many organizational guises, including HMOs, PPOs, IPAs, and managed health-insurance indemnity plans.

Managed competition. A plan for health care reform that would combine limited government regulation with free-market forces to reduce costs and increase access to care. Under this plan, consumers and businesses would form large groups (see *HIPC*) to buy health care from organized networks of doctors and hospitals that would compete to attract patients by offering the best quality at the lowest price.

Management-service organization (MSO). Any of a variety of business arrangements in which a hospital or entrepreneur contracts with physicians to manage their practices in exchange for part ownership or a percentage of overhead or revenues. The MSO markets the group to managed-care plans, but physicians themselves hold the contracts and provide the care.

Medical-foundation model. A tax-exempt entity—usually a hospital or clinic—that provides health care to patients. Physicians ally with foundations via professional services agreements. The foundation, not the doctor, holds the managed-care contracts.

Outcomes management. A system that encourages doctors to follow a set of guidelines (also called practice parameters or clinical paths) that research has shown to be the "one best way" to treat a medical ailment. Eventually, physicians' outcome records may be combined with their cost and quality-management profiles (see *economic credentialing*) and made public, to help consumers make informed decisions about quality care (see *outcomes research*).

Outcomes research. The attempt to determine which medical treatments get the best results. The goal is to standardize care and ensure predictable, desired outcomes in patients' health.

Physician-hospital organization (PHO). Loosely, any formal alliance between physicians and hospitals. PHOs are usually created for the purpose of managed-care contracting and to increase the organization's market share.

Point-of-service plan (POS). A health plan that allows patients to seek treatment at a member HMO or to consult doctors outside the plan for a higher deductible—for example, 70 percent reimbursement rather than 100 percent. Also called an HMO swing-out, or blended, plan.

Preferred-provider organization (PPO). An organization that contracts with "preferred" physicians who agree to provide health care to subscribers for a discounted fee. Some PPOs require doctors to put part of their discounted fee into a risk pool. They get all or part of this money back if their charges don't exceed an annual limit.

RB-RVS. The resource-based relative-value scale, a revised payment structure for the Medicare system that is intended to reward primary-care physicians and specialists more equitably than they have been in the past.

Single-payer system. A centralized system in which one payer, usually the government, pays all medical bills.

Vertically integrated system. A system that provides primary care, specialty care, and hospital care under one umbrella. Such systems are helpful in attracting managed-care contracts, and most experts believe all health-care providers will eventually organize themselves this way. Also called an integrated delivery system (IDS).

Additional Copies

To order copies of *Revolution* for friends or colleagues,
please write to The Grand Rounds Press, Whittle Books,
333 Main St., Knoxville, Tenn. 37902. Please include the recipient's name,
mailing address, and, where applicable, primary specialty and ME number.

For a single copy, please enclose a check for $21.95 plus $3.50 for postage and
handling, payable to The Grand Rounds Press. Quantities may be limited.
Discounts apply to bulk orders when available. To order by phone using your
MasterCard or Visa card, please call 800-765-5889.

Also available, at the same price, are copies of the previous books from
The Grand Rounds Press:

The Doctor Watchers by Spencer Vibbert
The New Genetics by Leon Jaroff
Surgeon Koop by Gregg Easterbrook
Inside Medical Washington by James H. Sammons, M.D.
Medicine For Sale by Richard Currey
The Doctor Dilemma by Gerald R. Weissmann, M.D.
Taking Care of Your Own by Perri Klass, M.D.
The Logic of Health-Care Reform by Paul Starr
Raising the Dead by Richard Selzer
Malpractice Solutions by James Rosenblum
What Works by Spencer Vibbert

Please allow four weeks for delivery.
Tennessee residents must add 8 ¼ percent sales tax.

Advertiser's Appendix

Prescribing Information as of October 1992 (2)

CARDIZEM® CD
(diltiazem HCl)
Capsules

DESCRIPTION

CARDIZEM® (diltiazem hydrochloride) is a calcium ion influx inhibitor (slow channel blocker or calcium antagonist). Chemically, diltiazem hydrochloride is 1,5-Benzothiazepin-4(5H)one,3-(acetyloxy)-5-[2-(dimethylamino)ethyl]-2,3-dihydro-2-(4-methoxyphenyl)-, monohydrochloride,(+)-cis-. The chemical structure is:

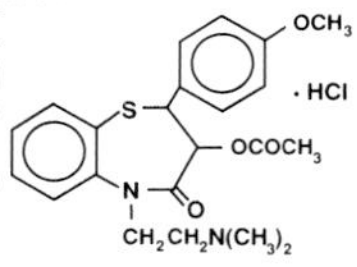

Diltiazem hydrochloride is a white to off-white crystalline powder with a bitter taste. It is soluble in water, methanol, and chloroform. It has a molecular weight of 450.98. CARDIZEM CD is formulated as a once-a-day extended release capsule containing either 120 mg, 180 mg, 240 mg, or 300 mg diltiazem hydrochloride.

Also contains: black iron oxide, ethylcellulose, FD&C Blue #1, fumaric acid, gelatin-NF, sucrose, starch, talc, titanium dioxide, white wax, and other ingredients.

For oral administration.

CLINICAL PHARMACOLOGY

The therapeutic effects of CARDIZEM CD are believed to be related to its ability to inhibit the influx of calcium ions during membrane depolarization of cardiac and vascular smooth muscle.

Mechanisms of Action.

Hypertension. CARDIZEM CD produces its antihypertensive effect primarily by relaxation of vascular smooth muscle and the resultant decrease in peripheral vascular resistance. The magnitude of blood pressure reduction is related to the degree of hypertension; thus hypertensive individuals experience an antihypertensive effect, whereas there is only a modest fall in blood pressure in normotensives.

Angina. CARDIZEM CD has been shown to produce increases in exercise tolerance, probably due to its ability to reduce myocardial oxygen demand. This is accomplished via reductions in heart rate and systemic blood pressure at submaximal and maximal work loads. Diltiazem has been shown to be a potent dilator of coronary arteries, both epicardial and subendocardial. Spontaneous and ergonovine-induced coronary artery spasm are inhibited by diltiazem.

In animal models, diltiazem interferes with the slow inward (depolarizing) current in excitable tissue. It causes excitation-contraction uncoupling in various myocardial tissues without changes in the configuration of the action potential. Diltiazem produces relaxation of coronary vascular smooth muscle and dilation of both large and small coronary arteries at drug levels which cause little or no negative inotropic effect. The resultant increases in coronary blood flow (epicardial and subendocardial) occur in ischemic and nonischemic models and are accompanied by dose-dependent decreases in systemic blood pressure and decreases in peripheral resistance.

Hemodynamic and Electrophysiologic Effects.

Like other calcium channel antagonists, diltiazem decreases sinoatrial and atrioventricular conduction in isolated tissues and has a negative inotropic effect in isolated preparations. In the intact animal, prolongation of the AH interval can be seen at higher doses.

In man, diltiazem prevents spontaneous and ergonovine-provoked coronary artery spasm. It causes a decrease in peripheral vascular resistance and a modest fall in blood pressure in normotensive individuals and, in exercise tolerance studies in patients with ischemic heart disease, reduces the heart rate-blood pressure product for any given work load. Studies to date, primarily in patients with good ventricular function, have not revealed evidence of a negative inotropic effect; cardiac output, ejection fraction, and left ventricular end diastolic pressure have not been affected. Such data have no predictive value with respect to effects in patients with poor ventricular function, and increased heart failure has been reported in patients with preexisting impairment of ventricular function. There are as yet few data on the interaction of diltiazem and beta-blockers in patients with poor ventricular function. Resting heart rate is usually slightly reduced by diltiazem.

In hypertensive patients, CARDIZEM CD produces antihypertensive effects both in the supine and standing positions. In a double-blind, parallel, dose-response study utilizing doses ranging from 90 to 540 mg once daily, CARDIZEM CD lowered supine diastolic blood pressure in an apparent linear manner over the entire dose range studied. The changes in diastolic blood pressure, measured at trough, for placebo, 90 mg, 180 mg, 360 mg, and 540 mg were -2.9, -4.5, -6.1, -9.5, and -10.5 mm Hg, respectively. Postural hypotension is infrequently noted upon suddenly assuming an upright position. No reflex tachycardia is associated with the chronic antihypertensive effects. CARDIZEM CD decreases vascular resistance, increases cardiac output (by increasing stroke volume), and produces a slight decrease or no change in heart rate. During dynamic exercise, increases in diastolic pressure are inhibited while maximum achievable systolic pressure is usually reduced. Chronic therapy with CARDIZEM CD produces no change or an increase in plasma catecholamines. No increased activity of the renin-angiotensin-aldosterone axis has been observed. CARDIZEM CD reduces the renal and peripheral effects of angiotensin II. Hypertensive animal models respond to diltiazem with reductions in blood pressure and increased urinary output and natriuresis without a change in urinary sodium/potassium ratio.

In a double-blind, parallel dose response study of doses from 60 mg to 480 mg once daily, CARDIZEM CD increased time to termination of exercise in a linear manner over the entire dose range studied. The improvement in time to termination of exercise utilizing a Bruce exercise protocol, measured at trough, for placebo, 60 mg, 120 mg, 240 mg, 360 mg, and 480 mg was 29, 40, 56, 51, 69 and 68 seconds, respectively. As doses of CARDIZEM CD were increased, overall angina frequency was decreased. CARDIZEM CD, 180 mg once daily, or placebo was administered in a double-blind study to patients receiving concomitant treatment with long-acting nitrates and/or beta-blockers. A significant increase in time to termination of exercise and a significant decrease in overall angina frequency was observed. In this trial the overall frequency of adverse events in the CARDIZEM CD treatment group was the same as the placebo group.

Intravenous diltiazem in doses of 20 mg prolongs AH conduction time and AV node functional and effective refractory periods by approximately 20%. In a study involving single oral doses of 300 mg of CARDIZEM in six normal volunteers, the average maximum PR prolongation was 14% with no instances of greater than first-degree AV block. Diltiazem-associated prolongation of the AH interval is not more pronounced in patients with first-degree heart block. In patients with sick sinus syndrome, diltiazem significantly prolongs sinus cycle length (up to 50% in some cases). Chronic oral administration of CARDIZEM to patients in doses of up to 540 mg/day has resulted in small increases in PR interval, and on occasion produces abnormal prolongation. (See WARNINGS.)

Pharmacokinetics and Metabolism.

Diltiazem is well absorbed from the gastrointestinal tract and is subject to an extensive first-pass effect, giving an absolute bioavailability (compared to intravenous administration) of about 40%. CARDIZEM undergoes extensive metabolism in which only 2% to 4% of the unchanged drug appears in the urine. Drugs which induce or inhibit hepatic microsomal enzymes may alter diltiazem disposition.

Total radioactivity measurement following short IV administration in healthy volunteers suggests the presence of other unidentified metabolites which attain higher concentrations than those of diltiazem and are more slowly eliminated; half-life of total radioactivity is about 20 hours compared to 2 to 5 hours for diltiazem.

In vitro binding studies show CARDIZEM is 70% to 80% bound to plasma proteins. Competitive in vitro ligand binding studies have also shown CARDIZEM binding is not altered by therapeutic concentrations of digoxin, hydrochlorothiazide, phenylbutazone, propranolol, salicylic acid, or warfarin. The plasma elimination half-life following single or multiple drug administration is approximately 3.0 to 4.5 hours. Desacetyl diltiazem is also present in the plasma at levels of 10% to 20% of the parent drug and is 25% to 50% as potent as a coronary vasodilator as diltiazem. Minimum therapeutic plasma diltiazem concentrations appear to be in the range of 50 to 200 ng/mL. There is a departure from linearity when dose strengths are increased; the half-life is slightly increased with dose. A study that compared patients with normal hepatic function to patients with cirrhosis found an increase in half-life and a 69% increase in bioavailability in the hepatically impaired patients. A single study in patients with severely impaired renal function showed no difference in the pharmacokinetic profile of diltiazem compared to patients with normal renal function.

CARDIZEM CD Capsules. When compared to a regimen of CARDIZEM tablets at steady-state, more than 95% of drug is absorbed from the CARDIZEM CD formulation. A single 360-mg dose of the capsule results in detectable plasma levels within 2 hours and peak plasma levels between 10 and 14 hours; absorption occurs throughout the dosing interval. When CARDIZEM CD was coadministered with a high fat content breakfast, the extent of diltiazem absorption was not affected. Dose-dumping does not occur. The apparent elimination half-life after single or multiple dosing is 5 to 8 hours. A departure from linearity similar to that seen with CARDIZEM tablets and CARDIZEM SR capsules is observed. As the dose of CARDIZEM CD capsules is increased from a daily dose of 120 mg to 240 mg, there is an increase in the area-under-the-curve of 2.7 times. When the dose is increased from 240 mg to 360 mg there is an increase in the area-under-the-curve of 1.6 times.

INDICATIONS AND USAGE

CARDIZEM CD is indicated for the treatment of hypertension. It may be used alone or in combination with other antihypertensive medications.

CARDIZEM CD is indicated for the management of chronic stable angina and angina due to coronary artery spasm.

CONTRAINDICATIONS

CARDIZEM is contraindicated in (1) patients with sick sinus syndrome except in the presence of a functioning ventricular pacemaker, (2) patients with second- or third-degree AV block except in the presence of a functioning ventricular pacemaker, (3) patients with hypotension (less than 90 mm Hg systolic), (4) patients who have demonstrated hypersensitivity to the drug, and (5) patients with acute myocardial infarction and pulmonary congestion documented by x-ray on admission.

WARNINGS

1. **Cardiac Conduction.** CARDIZEM prolongs AV node refractory periods without significantly prolonging sinus node recovery time, except in patients with sick sinus syndrome. This effect may rarely result in abnormally slow heart rates (particularly in patients with sick sinus syndrome) or second- or third-degree AV block (13 of 3,290 patients or 0.40%). Concomitant use of diltiazem with beta-blockers or digitalis may result in additive effects on cardiac conduction. A patient with Prinzmetal's angina developed periods of asystole (2 to 5 seconds) after a single dose of 60 mg of diltiazem.
2. **Congestive Heart Failure.** Although diltiazem has a negative inotropic effect in isolated animal tissue preparations, hemodynamic studies in humans with normal ventricular function have not shown a reduction in cardiac index nor consistent negative effects on contractility (dp/dt). An acute study of oral diltiazem in patients with impaired ventricular function (ejection fraction 24% ± 6%) showed improvement in indices of ventricular function without significant decrease in contractile function (dp/dt). Worsening of congestive heart failure has been reported in patients with preexisting impairment of ventricular function. Experience with the use of CARDIZEM (diltiazem hydrochloride) in combination with beta-blockers in patients with impaired ventricular function is limited. Caution should be exercised when using this combination.
3. **Hypotension.** Decreases in blood pressure associated with CARDIZEM therapy may occasionally result in symptomatic hypotension.
4. **Acute Hepatic Injury.** Mild elevations of transaminases with and without concomitant elevation in alkaline phosphatase and bilirubin have been observed in clinical studies. Such elevations were usually transient and frequently resolved even with continued diltiazem treatment. In rare instances, significant elevations in enzymes such as alkaline phosphatase, LDH, SGOT, SGPT, and other phenomena consistent with acute hepatic injury have been noted. These reactions tended to occur early after therapy initiation (1 to 8 weeks) and have been reversible upon discontinuation of drug therapy. The relationship to CARDIZEM is uncertain in some cases, but probable in some. (See PRECAUTIONS.)

PRECAUTIONS

General.

CARDIZEM (diltiazem hydrochloride) is extensively metabolized by the liver and excreted by the kidneys and in bile. As with any drug given over prolonged periods, laboratory parameters of renal and hepatic function should be monitored at regular intervals. The drug should be used with caution in patients with impaired renal or hepatic function. In subacute and chronic dog and rat studies designed to produce toxicity, high doses of diltiazem were associated with hepatic damage. In special subacute hepatic studies, oral doses of 125 mg/kg and higher in rats were associated with histological changes in the liver which were reversible when the drug was discontinued. In dogs, doses of 20 mg/kg were also associated with hepatic changes; however, these changes were reversible with continued dosing.

Dermatological events (see ADVERSE REACTIONS section) may be transient and may disappear despite continued use of CARDIZEM. However, skin eruptions progressing to erythema multiforme and/or exfoliative dermatitis have also been infrequently reported. Should a dermatologic reaction persist, the drug should be discontinued.

Drug Interactions.

Due to the potential for additive effects, caution and careful titration are warranted in patients receiving CARDIZEM concomitantly with other agents known to affect cardiac contractility and/or conduction. (See WARNINGS.) Pharmacologic studies indicate that there may be additive effects in prolonging AV conduction when using beta-blockers or digitalis concomitantly with CARDIZEM. (See WARNINGS.)

As with all drugs, care should be exercised when treating patients with multiple medications. CARDIZEM undergoes biotransformation by cytochrome P-450 mixed function oxidase. Coadministration of CARDIZEM with other agents which follow the same route of biotransformation may result in the competitive inhibition of metabolism. Dosages of similarly metabolized drugs such as cyclosporin, particularly those of low therapeutic ratio or in patients with renal and/or hepatic impairment, may require adjustment when starting or stopping concomitantly administered CARDIZEM to maintain optimum therapeutic blood levels.

Beta-blockers. Controlled and uncontrolled domestic studies suggest that concomitant use of CARDIZEM and beta-blockers is usually well tolerated, but available data are not sufficient to predict the effects of concomitant treatment in patients with left ventricular dysfunction or cardiac conduction abnormalities.

Administration of CARDIZEM (diltiazem hydrochloride) concomitantly with propranolol in five normal volunteers resulted in increased propranolol levels in all subjects and bioavailability of propranolol was increased approximately 50%. In vitro, propranolol appears to be displaced from its binding sites by diltiazem. If combination therapy is initiated or withdrawn in conjunction with propranolol, an adjustment in the propranolol dose may be warranted. (See WARNINGS.)

Cimetidine. A study in six healthy volunteers has shown a significant increase in peak diltiazem plasma levels (58%) and area-under-the-curve (53%) after a 1-week course of cimetidine at 1200 mg per day and a single dose of diltiazem 60 mg. Ranitidine produced smaller, nonsignificant increases. The effect may be mediated by cimetidine's known inhibition of hepatic cytochrome P-450, the enzyme system responsible for the first-pass metabolism of diltiazem. Patients currently receiving diltiazem therapy should be carefully monitored for a change in pharmacological effect when initiating and discontinuing therapy with cimetidine. An adjustment in the diltiazem dose may be warranted.

Digitalis. Administration of CARDIZEM with digoxin in 24 healthy male subjects increased plasma digoxin concentrations approximately 20%. Another investigator found no increase in digoxin levels in 12 patients with coronary artery disease. Since there have been conflicting results regarding the effect of digoxin levels, it is recommended that digoxin levels be monitored when initiating, adjusting, and discontinuing CARDIZEM therapy to avoid possible over- or under-digitalization. (See WARNINGS.)

Anesthetics. The depression of cardiac contractility, conductivity, and automaticity as well as the vascular dilation associated with anesthetics may be potentiated by calcium channel blockers. When used concomitantly, anesthetics and calcium blockers should be titrated carefully.

Carcinogenesis, Mutagenesis, Impairment of Fertility.

A 24-month study in rats at oral dosage levels of up to 100 mg/kg/day and a 21-month study in mice at oral dosage levels of up to 30 mg/kg/day showed no evidence of carcinogenicity. There was also no mutagenic response in vitro or in vivo in mammalian cell assays or in vitro in bacteria. No evidence of impaired fertility was observed in a study performed in male and female rats at oral dosages of up to 100 mg/kg/day.

Pregnancy.

Category C. Reproduction studies have been conducted in mice, rats, and rabbits. Administration of doses ranging from five to ten times greater (on a mg/kg basis) than the daily recommended therapeutic dose has resulted in embryo and fetal lethality. These doses, in some studies, have been reported to cause skeletal abnormalities. In the perinatal/postnatal studies, there was an increased incidence of stillbirths at doses of 20 times the human dose or greater.

There are no well-controlled studies in pregnant women; therefore, use CARDIZEM in pregnant women only if the potential benefit justifies the potential risk to the fetus.

Nursing Mothers. Diltiazem is excreted in human milk. One report suggests that concentrations in breast milk may approximate serum levels. If use of CARDIZEM is deemed essential, an alternative method of infant feeding should be instituted.

Pediatric Use. Safety and effectiveness in children have not been established.

ADVERSE REACTIONS

Serious adverse reactions have been rare in studies carried out to date, but it should be recognized that patients with impaired ventricular function and cardiac conduction abnormalities have usually been excluded from these studies.

The following table presents the most common adverse reactions reported in placebo-controlled angina and hypertension trials in patients receiving CARDIZEM CD up to 360 mg with rates in placebo patients shown for comparison.

CARDIZEM CD Capsule Placebo-Controlled Angina and Hypertension Trials Combined

Adverse Reaction	Cardizem CD N=607	Placebo N=301
Headache	5.4%	5.0%
Dizziness	3.0%	3.0%
Bradycardia	3.3%	1.3%
AV Block First Degree	3.3%	0.0%
Edema	2.6%	1.3%
ECG Abnormality	1.6%	2.3%
Asthenia	1.8%	1.7%

In clinical trials of CARDIZEM CD Capsules, CARDIZEM Tablets, and CARDIZEM SR Capsules involving over 3200 patients, the most common events (ie, greater than 1%) were edema (4.6%), headache (4.6%), dizziness (3.5%), asthenia (2.6%), first-degree AV block (2.4%), bradycardia (1.7%), flushing (1.4%), nausea (1.4%), and rash (1.2%). In addition, the following events were reported infrequently (less than 1%) in angina or hypertension trials:

Cardiovascular: Angina, arrhythmia, AV block (second- or third-degree), bundle branch block, congestive heart failure, ECG abnormalities, hypotension, palpitations, syncope, tachycardia, ventricular extrasystoles

Nervous System: Abnormal dreams, amnesia, depression, gait abnormality, hallucinations, insomnia, nervousness, paresthesia, personality change, somnolence, tinnitus, tremor

Gastrointestinal: Anorexia, constipation, diarrhea, dry mouth, dysgeusia, dyspepsia, mild elevations of SGOT, SGPT, LDH, and alkaline phosphatase (see hepatic warnings), thirst, vomiting, weight increase

Dermatological: Petechiae, photosensitivity, pruritus, urticaria

Other: Amblyopia, CPK increase, dyspnea, epistaxis, eye irritation, hyperglycemia, hyperuricemia, impotence, muscle cramps, nasal congestion, nocturia, osteoarticular pain, polyuria, sexual difficulties

The following postmarketing events have been reported infrequently in patients receiving CARDIZEM: alopecia, erythema multiforme, exfoliative dermatitis, extrapyramidal symptoms, gingival hyperplasia, hemolytic anemia, increased bleeding time, leukopenia, purpura, retinopathy, and thrombocytopenia. In addition, events such as myocardial infarction have been observed which are not readily distinguishable from the natural history of the disease in these patients. A number of well-documented cases of generalized rash, characterized as leukocytoclastic vasculitis, have been reported. However, a definitive cause and effect relationship between these events and CARDIZEM therapy is yet to be established.

OVERDOSAGE

The oral LD_{50}'s in mice and rats range from 415 to 740 mg/kg and from 560 to 810 mg/kg, respectively. The intravenous LD_{50}'s in these species were 60 and 38 mg/kg, respectively. The oral LD_{50} in dogs is considered to be in excess of 50 mg/kg, while lethality was seen in monkeys at 360 mg/kg.

The toxic dose in man is not known. Due to extensive metabolism, blood levels after a standard dose of diltiazem can vary over tenfold, limiting the usefulness of blood levels in overdose cases.

There have been 29 reports of diltiazem overdose in doses ranging from less than 1 gm to 10.8 gm. Sixteen of these reports involved multiple drug ingestions.

Twenty-two reports indicated patients had recovered from diltiazem overdose ranging from less than 1 gm to 10.8 gm. There were seven reports with a fatal outcome, although the amount of diltiazem ingested was unknown, multiple drug ingestions were confirmed in six of the seven reports.

Events observed following diltiazem overdose included bradycardia, hypotension, heart block, and cardiac failure. Most reports of overdose described some supportive medical measure and/or drug treatment. Bradycardia frequently responded favorably to atropine as did heart block, although cardiac pacing was also frequently utilized to treat heart block. Fluids and vasopressors were used to maintain blood pressure, and in cases of cardiac failure, inotropic agents were administered. In addition, some patients received treatment with ventilatory support, gastric lavage, activated charcoal, and/or intravenous calcium. Evidence of the effectiveness of intravenous calcium administration to reverse the pharmacological effects of diltiazem overdose was conflicting.

In the event of overdose or exaggerated response, appropriate supportive measures should be employed in addition to gastrointestinal decontamination. Diltiazem does not appear to be removed by peritoneal or hemodialysis. Based on the known pharmacological effects of diltiazem and/or reported clinical experiences, the following measures may be considered:

Bradycardia: Administer atropine (0.60 to 1.0 mg). If there is no response to vagal blockade, administer isoproterenol cautiously

High-degree AV Block: Treat as for bradycardia above. Fixed high-degree AV block should be treated with cardiac pacing

Cardiac Failure: Administer inotropic agents (isoproterenol, dopamine, or dobutamine) and diuretics

Hypotension: Vasopressors (eg, dopamine or levarterenol bitartrate)

Actual treatment and dosage should depend on the severity of the clinical situation and the judgment and experience of the treating physician.

DOSAGE AND ADMINISTRATION

Patients controlled on diltiazem alone or in combination with other medications may be safely switched to CARDIZEM CD capsules at the nearest equivalent total daily dose. Subsequent titration to higher or lower doses may be necessary and should be initiated as clinically warranted. There is limited general clinical experience with doses above 360 mg, but doses to 540 mg have been studied in clinical trials. The incidence of side effects increases as the dose increases with first-degree AV block, dizziness and sinus bradycardia bearing the strongest relationship to dose.

Hypertension: Dosage needs to be adjusted by titration to individual patient needs. When used as monotherapy, reasonable starting doses are 180 to 240 mg once daily, although some patients may respond to lower doses. Maximum antihypertenisve effect is usually observed by 14 days of chronic therapy; therefore, dosage adjustments should be scheduled accordingly. The usual dosage range studied in clinical trials was 240 to 360 mg once daily. Individual patients may respond to higher doses of up to 480 mg once daily.

Angina: Dosages for the treatment of angina should be adjusted to each patient's needs, starting with a dose of 120 or 180 mg once daily. Individual patients may respond to higher doses of up to 480 mg once daily. When necessary, titration may be carried out over a 7 to 14 day period.

Concomitant Use With Other Cardiovascular Agents

1. **Sublingual NTG** may be taken as required to abort acute anginal attacks during CARDIZEM CD (diltiazem hydrochloride) therapy.

2. **Prophylactic Nitrate Therapy**—CARDIZEM CD may be safely coadministered with short- and long-acting nitrates.

3. **Beta-blockers**. (See WARNINGS and PRECAUTIONS.)

4. **Antihypertensives**—CARDIZEM CD has an additive antihypertensive effect when used with other antihypertensive agents. Therefore, the dosage of CARDIZEM CD or the concomitant antihypertensives may need to be adjusted when adding one to the other.

HOW SUPPLIED

CARDIZEM® CD
(diltiazem hydrochloride)
Capsules

Strength	Quantity	NDC Number	Description
120 mg	30 btl 90 btl 100 UDIP	0088-1795-30 0088-1795-42 0088-1795-49	Light turquoise blue/light turquoise blue capsule imprinted with the Marion Merrell Dow Inc. logo on one end and CARDIZEM CD and 120 mg on the other.
180 mg	30 btl 90 btl 100 UDIP	0088-1796-30 0088-1796-42 0088-1796-49	Light turquoise blue/blue capsule imprinted with the Marion Merrell Dow Inc. logo on one end and CARDIZEM CD and 180 mg on the other.
240 mg	30 btl 90 btl 100 UDIP	0088-1797-30 0088-1797-42 0088-1797-49	Blue/blue capsule imprinted with the Marion Merrell Dow Inc. logo on one end and CARDIZEM CD and 240 mg on the other.
300 mg	30 btl 90 btl 100 UDIP	0088-1798-30 0088-1798-42 0088-1798-49	Light gray/blue capsule imprinted with the Marion Merrell Dow Inc. logo on one end and CARDIZEM CD and 300 mg on the other.

Storage Conditions: Store at controlled room temperature 59-86° F (15-30°C).
Avoid excessive humidity.

Prescribing Information as of October 1992 (2)

Marion Merrell Dow Inc.
Kansas City, MO 64114

ccdp1092(2)e

Prescribing Information as of January 1993

SELDANE®
(terfenadine)
60 mg Tablets

WARNING BOX
QT INTERVAL PROLONGATION/VENTRICULAR ARRHYTHMIA

RARE CASES OF SERIOUS CARDIOVASCULAR ADVERSE EVENTS, INCLUDING DEATH, CARDIAC ARREST, TORSADES DE POINTES, AND OTHER VENTRICULAR ARRHYTHMIAS, HAVE BEEN OBSERVED IN THE FOLLOWING CLINICAL SETTINGS, FREQUENTLY IN ASSOCIATION WITH INCREASED TERFENADINE LEVELS WHICH LEAD TO ELECTROCARDIOGRAPHIC QT PROLONGATION:

1. **CONCOMITANT ADMINISTRATION OF KETOCONAZOLE (NIZORAL) OR ITRACONAZOLE (SPORANOX)**
2. **OVERDOSE, INCLUDING SINGLE DOSES AS LOW AS 360 MG**
3. **CONCOMITANT ADMINISTRATION OF CLARITHROMYCIN, ERYTHROMYCIN, OR TROLEANDOMYCIN**
4. **SIGNIFICANT HEPATIC DYSFUNCTION**

TERFENADINE IS CONTRAINDICATED IN PATIENTS TAKING KETOCONAZOLE, ITRACONAZOLE, ERYTHROMYCIN, CLARITHROMYCIN, OR TROLEANDOMYCIN, AND IN PATIENTS WITH SIGNIFICANT HEPATIC DYSFUNCTION.

DO NOT EXCEED RECOMMENDED DOSE.

IN SOME CASES, SEVERE ARRHYTHMIAS HAVE BEEN PRECEDED BY EPISODES OF SYNCOPE. SYNCOPE IN PATIENTS RECEIVING TERFENADINE SHOULD LEAD TO DISCONTINUATION OF TREATMENT AND FULL EVALUATION OF POTENTIAL ARRHYTHMIAS.

(See CONTRAINDICATIONS, WARNINGS, CLINICAL PHARMACOLOGY, AND PRECAUTIONS: DRUG INTERACTIONS.)

DESCRIPTION

SELDANE (terfenadine) is available as tablets for oral administration. Each tablet contains 60 mg terfenadine. Tablets also contain, as inactive ingredients: corn starch, gelatin, lactose, magnesium stearate, and sodium bicarbonate.

Terfenadine is a histamine H_1-receptor antagonist with the chemical name α-[4-(1,1-Dimethylethyl) phenyl]-4-(hydroxydiphenylmethyl)-1-piperidinebutanol (±). The molecular weight is 471.68. The molecular formula is $C_{32}H_{41}NO_2$.

It has the following chemical structure:

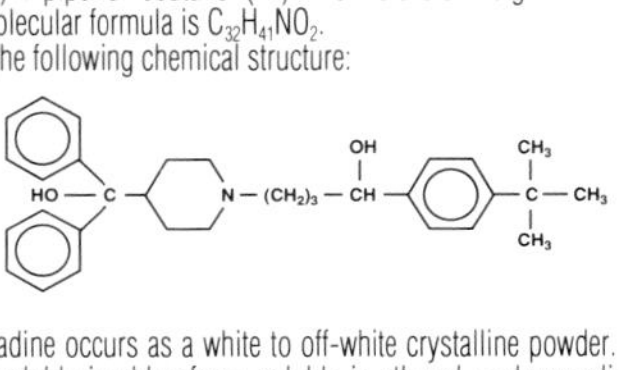

Terfenadine occurs as a white to off-white crystalline powder. It is freely soluble in chloroform, soluble in ethanol, and very slightly soluble in water.

CLINICAL PHARMACOLOGY

Terfenadine is chemically distinct from other antihistamines.

Histamine skin wheal studies have shown that SELDANE in single and repeated doses of 60 mg in 64 subjects has an antihistaminic effect beginning at 1-2 hours, reaching its maximum at 3-4 hours, and lasting in excess of 12 hours. The correlation between response on skin wheal testing and clinical efficacy is unclear. The four best controlled and largest clinical trials each lasted 7 days and involved about 1,000 total patients in comparisons of SELDANE (60 mg b.i.d.) with an active drug (chlorpheniramine, 4 mg t.i.d.; dexchlorpheniramine, 2 mg t.i.d.; or clemastine 1 mg b.i.d.). About 50-70% of SELDANE or other antihistamine recipients had moderate to complete relief of symptoms, compared with 30-50% of placebo recipients. The frequency of drowsiness with SELDANE was similar to the frequency with placebo and less than with other antihistamines. None of these studies showed a difference between SELDANE and other antihistamines in the frequency of anticholinergic effects. In studies which included 52 subjects in whom EEG assessments were made, no depressant effects have been observed.

Animal studies have demonstrated that terfenadine is a histamine H_1-receptor antagonist. In these animal studies, no sedative or anticholinergic effects were observed at effective antihistaminic doses. Radioactive disposition and autoradiographic studies in rats and radioligand binding studies with guinea pig brain H_1-receptors indicate that, at effective antihistamine doses, neither terfenadine nor its metabolites penetrate the blood brain barrier well.

On the basis of a mass balance study using ^{14}C labeled terfenadine the oral absorption of terfen-adine was estimated to be at least 70%. Terfenadine itself undergoes extensive (99%) first pass metabolism to two primary metabolites, an active acid metabolite and an inactive dealkylated metabolite. Therefore, systemic availability of terfenadine is low under normal conditions, and parent terfenadine is not normally detectable in plasma at levels >10 ng/mL. Although in rare cases there was measurable plasma terfenadine in apparently normal individuals without identifiable risk factors, the implications of this finding with respect to the variability of terfenadine metabolism in the normal population cannot be assessed without further study. Further studies of terfenadine metabolism in the general population are pending. From information gained in the ^{14}C study it appears that approximately forty percent of the total dose is eliminated renally (40% as acid metabolite, 30% dealkyl metabolite, and 30% minor unidentified metabolites). Sixty percent of the dose is eliminated in the feces (50% as the acid metabolite, 2% unchanged terfenadine, and the remainder as minor unidentified metabolites). Studies investigating the effect of hepatic and renal insufficiency on the metabolism and excretion of terfenadine are incomplete. Preliminary information indicates that in cases of hepatic impairment, significant concentrations of unchanged terfenadine can be detected with the rate of acid metabolite formation being decreased. A single-dose study in patients with hepatic impairment revealed increased parent terfenadine and impaired metabolism, suggesting that additional drug accumulation may occur after repetitive dosing in such patients. Terfenadine is contraindicated for use in patients with significant hepatic dysfunction. (See CONTRAINDICATIONS and WARNINGS.) In subjects with normal hepatic function, unchanged terfenadine plasma concentrations have not been detected. **Elevated levels of parent terfenadine, whether due to significant hepatic dysfunction, concomitant medications, or overdose, have been associated with QT interval prolongation and serious cardiac adverse events.** (See CONTRAINDICATIONS and WARNINGS.) In controlled clinical trials in otherwise normal patients with rhinitis, small increases in QTc interval were observed at doses of 60 mg b.i.d. In studies at 300 mg b.i.d. a mean increase in QTc of 10% (range −4% to +30%) (mean increase of 46 msec) was observed.

Data have been reported demonstrating that compared to young subjects, elderly subjects experience a 25% reduction in clearance of the acid metabolite after single-dose oral administration of 120 mg. Further studies are necessary to fully characterize pharmacokinetics in the elderly.

In vitro studies demonstrate that terfenadine is extensively (97%) bound to human serum protein while the acid metabolite is approximately 70% bound to human serum protein. Based on data gathered from in vitro models of antihistaminic activity, the acid metabolite of terfenadine has approximately 30% of the H_1 blocking activity of terfenadine. The relative contribution of terfenadine and the acid metabolite to the pharmacodynamic effects have not been clearly defined. Since unchanged terfenadine is usually not detected in plasma, and active acid metabolite concentrations are relatively high, the acid metabolite may be the entity responsible for the majority of efficacy after oral administration of terfenadine.

In a study involving the administration of a single 60 mg SELDANE tablet to 24 subjects, mean peak plasma levels of the acid metabolite were 263 ng/mL (range 133-423 ng/mL) and occurred approximately 2.5 hours after dosing. Plasma concentrations of unchanged terfenadine were not detected. The elimination profile of the acid metabolite was biphasic in nature with an initial mean plasma half-life of 3.5 hours followed by a mean plasma half-life of 6 hours. Ninety percent of the plasma level time curve was associated with these half-lives. Although the elimination profile is somewhat complex, the effective pharmacokinetic half-life can be estimated at approximately 8.5 hours. However, receptor binding and pharmacologic effects, both therapeutic and adverse, may persist well beyond that time.

INDICATIONS AND USAGE

SELDANE is indicated for the relief of symptoms associated with seasonal allergic rhinitis such as sneezing, rhinorrhea, pruritus, and lacrimation.

Clinical studies conducted to date have not demonstrated effectiveness of terfenadine in the common cold.

CONTRAINDICATIONS

CONCOMITANT ADMINISTRATION OF TERFENADINE WITH KETOCONAZOLE (NIZORAL) OR ITRACONAZOLE (SPORANOX) IS CONTRAINDICATED. TERFENADINE IS ALSO CONTRAINDICATED IN PATIENTS WITH DISEASE STATES OR OTHER CONCOMITANT MEDICATIONS KNOWN TO IMPAIR ITS METABOLISM, INCLUDING SIGNIFICANT HEPATIC DYSFUNCTION, AND CONCURRENT USE OF CLARITHROMYCIN, ERYTHROMYCIN, OR TROLEANDOMYCIN. QT PROLONGATION HAS BEEN DEMONSTRATED IN SOME PATIENTS TAKING TERFENADINE IN THESE SETTINGS, AND RARE CASES OF SERIOUS CARDIOVASCULAR EVENTS, INCLUDING DEATH, CARDIAC ARREST, AND TORSADES DE POINTES, HAVE BEEN REPORTED IN THESE PATIENT POPULATIONS. (See WARNINGS and PRECAUTIONS: Drug Interactions.)

SELDANE is contraindicated in patients with a known hypersensitivity to terfenadine or any of its ingredients.

WARNINGS

Terfenadine undergoes extensive metabolism in the liver by a specific cytochrome P-450 isoenzyme. This metabolic pathway may be impaired in patients with hepatic dysfunction (alcoholic cirrhosis, hepatitis) or who are taking drugs such as ketoconazole, itraconazole, or clarithromycin, erythromycin, or troleandomycin (macrolide antibiotics), or other potent inhibitors of this isoenzyme. Interference with this metabolism can lead to elevated terfenadine plasma levels associated with QT prolongation and increased risk of ventricular tachyarrhythmias (such as torsades de pointes, ventricular tachycardia, and ventricular fibrillation) at the recommended dose. SELDANE is contraindicated for use by patients with these conditions (see WARNING BOX, CONTRAINDICATIONS, and PRECAUTIONS: Drug Interactions).

Other patients who may be at risk for these adverse cardiovascular events include patients who may experience new or increased QT prolongation while receiving certain drugs or having conditions which lead to QT prolongation. These include patients taking certain antiarrhythmics, bepridil, certain psychotropics, probucol, or astemizole; patients with electrolyte abnormalities such as hypokalemia or hypomagnesemia, or taking diuretics with potential for inducing electrolyte abnormalities; and patients with congenital QT syndrome. SELDANE is not recommended for use by patients with these conditions.

The relationship of underlying cardiac disease to the development of ventricular tachyarrhythmias while on SELDANE therapy is unclear; nonetheless, SELDANE should also be used with caution in these patients.

PRECAUTIONS

Information for Patients

Patients taking SELDANE should receive the following information and instructions. Antihistamines are prescribed to reduce allergic symptoms. Patients should be advised to take SELDANE only as needed and NOT TO EXCEED THE PRESCRIBED DOSE. Patients should be questioned about use of any other prescription or over-the-counter medication, and should be cautioned regarding the potential for life-threatening arrhythmias with concurrent use of ketoconazole, itraconazole, clarithromycin, erythromycin, or troleandomycin. Patients should be advised to consult the physician before concurrent use of other medications with terfenadine. Patients should be questioned about pregnancy or lactation before starting SELDANE therapy, since the drug should be used in pregnancy or lactation only if the potential benefit justifies the potential risk to fetus or baby. Patients should also be instructed to store this medication in a tightly closed container in a cool, dry place, away from heat or direct sunlight, and away from children.

Drug Interactions

Ketoconazole

Spontaneous adverse reaction reports of patients taking concomitant ketoconazole with recommended doses of terfenadine demonstrate QT interval prolongation and rare serious cardiac events, e.g. death, cardiac arrest, and ventricular arrhythmia including torsades de pointes. Pharmacokinetic data indicate that ketoconazole markedly inhibits the metabolism of terfenadine, resulting in elevated plasma terfenadine levels. Presence of unchanged terfenadine is associated with statistically significant prolongation of the QT and QTc intervals. **Concomitant administration of ketoconazole and terfenadine is contraindicated** (see CONTRAINDICATIONS, WARNINGS, and ADVERSE REACTIONS).

Itraconazole

Torsades de pointes and elevated parent terfenadine levels have been reported during concomitant use of terfenadine and itraconazole in clinical trials of itraconazole and from foreign post-marketing sources. One death has also been reported from foreign post-marketing sources. **Concomitant administration of itraconazole and terfenadine is contraindicated** (see CONTRAINDICATIONS, WARNINGS, and ADVERSE REACTIONS.)

Due to the chemical similarity of other azole-type antifungal agents (including fluconazole, metronidazole, and miconazole) to ketoconazole and itraconazole, concomitant use of these products with terfenadine is not recommended pending full examination of potential interactions.

Macrolides

Clinical drug interaction studies indicate that erythromycin and clarithromycin can exert an effect on terfenadine metabolism by a mechanism which may be similar to that of ketoconazole, but to a lesser extent. Although erythromycin measurably decreases the clearance of the terfenadine acid metabolite, its influence on terfenadine plasma levels is still under investigation. A few spontaneous accounts of QT interval prolongation with ventricular arrhythmia, including torsades de pointes, have been reported in patients receiving erythromycin or troleandomycin.

Concomitant administration of terfenadine with clarithromycin, erythromycin, or troleandomycin is contraindicated (see CONTRAINDICATIONS, WARNINGS, and ADVERSE REACTIONS). Pending full characterization of potential interactions, concomitant administration of terfenadine with other macrolide antibiotics, including azithromycin, is not recommended. Studies to evaluate the potential interaction of terfenadine with azithromycin are in progress.

Carcinogenesis, Mutagenesis, Impairment of Fertility

Oral doses of terfenadine, corresponding to 63 times the recommended human daily dose, in mice for 18 months or in rats for 24 months, revealed no evidence of tumorigenicity. Microbial and micronucleus test assays with terfenadine have revealed no evidence of mutagenesis.

Reproduction and fertility studies in rats showed no effects on male or female fertility at oral doses of up to 21 times the human daily dose. At 63 times the human daily dose there was a small but significant reduction in implants and at 125 times the human daily dose reduced implants and increased post-implantation losses were observed, which were judged to be secondary to maternal toxicity.

Pregnancy Category C

There was no evidence of animal teratogenicity. Reproduction studies have been performed in rats at doses 63 times and 125 times the human daily dose and have revealed decreased pup weight gain and survival when terfenadine was administered throughout pregnancy and lactation. There are no adequate and well-controlled studies in pregnant women. SELDANE should be used during pregnancy only if the potential benefit justifies the potential risk to the fetus.

Nonteratogenic Effects

SELDANE is not recommended for nursing women. The drug has caused decreased pup weight gain and survival in rats given doses 63 times and 125 times the human daily dose throughout pregnancy and lactation. Effects on pups exposed to SELDANE only during lactation are not known, and there are no adequate and well-controlled studies in women during lactation.

Pediatric Use

Safety and effectiveness of SELDANE in children below the age of 12 years have not been established.

ADVERSE REACTIONS
Cardiovascular Adverse Events

Rare reports of severe cardiovascular adverse effects have been received which include ventricular tachyarrhythmias (torsades de pointes, ventricular tachycardia, ventricular fibrillation, and cardiac arrest), hypotension, palpitations, syncope, and dizziness. Rare reports of deaths resulting from ventricular tachyarrhythmias have been received (see CONTRAINDICATIONS, WARNINGS, and PRECAUTIONS: Drug Interactions). Hypotension, palpitations, syncope, and dizziness could reflect undetected ventricular arrhythmia. IN SOME PATIENTS, DEATH, CARDIAC ARREST, OR TORSADES DE POINTES HAVE BEEN PRECEDED BY EPISODES OF SYNCOPE. (See WARNING BOX.) Rare reports of serious cardiovascular adverse events have been received, some involving QT prolongation and torsades de pointes, in apparently normal individuals without identifiable risk factors; there is not conclusive evidence of a causal relationship of these events with terfenadine. Although in rare cases there was measurable plasma terfenadine, the implications of this finding with respect to the variability of terfenadine metabolism in the normal population cannot be assessed without further study. In controlled clinical trials in otherwise normal patients with rhinitis, small increases in QTc interval were observed at doses of 60 mg b.i.d. In studies at 300 mg b.i.d. a mean increase in QTc of 10% (range –4% to +30%) (mean increase of 46 msec) was observed.

General Adverse Events

Experience from clinical studies, including both controlled and uncontrolled studies involving more than 2,400 patients who received SELDANE, provides information on adverse experience incidence for periods of a few days up to six months. The usual dose in these studies was 60 mg twice daily, but in a small number of patients, the dose was as low as 20 mg twice a day, or as high as 600 mg daily.

In controlled clinical studies using the recommended dose of 60 mg b.i.d., the incidence of reported adverse effects in patients receiving SELDANE was similar to that reported in patients receiving placebo. (See Table below.)

Adverse Events Reported in Clinical Trials					
	Percent of Patients Reporting				
	Controlled Studies*			All Clinical Studies**	
Adverse Event	SELDANE N=781	Placebo N=665	Control N=626***	SELDANE N=2462	Placebo N=1478
Central Nervous System					
Drowsiness	9.0	8.1	18.1	8.5	8.2
Headache	6.3	7.4	3.8	15.8	11.2
Fatigue	2.9	0.9	5.8	4.5	3.0
Dizziness	1.4	1.1	1.0	1.5	1.2
Nervousness	0.9	0.2	0.6	1.7	1.0
Weakness	0.9	0.6	0.2	0.6	0.5
Appetite Increase	0.6	0.0	0.0	0.5	0.0
Gastrointestinal System					
Gastrointestinal Distress (Abdominal distress, Nausea, Vomiting, Change in bowel habits)	4.6	3.0	2.7	7.6	5.4
Eye, Ear, Nose, and Throat					
Dry Mouth/Nose/Throat	2.3	1.8	3.5	4.8	3.1
Cough	0.9	0.2	0.5	2.5	1.7
Sore Throat	0.5	0.3	0.5	3.2	1.6
Epistaxis	0.0	0.8	0.2	0.7	0.4
Skin					
Eruption (including rash and urticaria) or itching	1.0	1.7	1.4	1.6	2.0

* Duration of treatment in "CONTROLLED STUDIES" was usually 7-14 days.
** Duration of treatment in "ALL CLINICAL STUDIES" was up to 6 months.
*** CONTROL DRUGS: Chlorpheniramine (291 patients), d-Chlorpheniramine (189 patients), Clemastine (146 patients)

In addition to the more frequent side effects reported in clinical trials (See Table), adverse effects have been reported at a lower incidence in clinical trials and/or spontaneously during marketing of SELDANE that warrant listing as possibly associated with drug administration. These include: alopecia (hair loss or thinning), anaphylaxis, angioedema, bronchospasm, confusion, depression, galactorrhea, insomnia, menstrual disorders (including dysmenorrhea), musculoskeletal symptoms, nightmares, paresthesia, photosensitivity, rapid flare of psoriasis, seizures, sinus tachycardia, sweating, thrombocytopenia, tremor, urinary frequency, and visual disturbances.

In clinical trials, several instances of mild, or in one case, moderate transaminase elevations were seen in patients receiving SELDANE. Mild elevations were also seen in placebo treated patients. Marketing experiences include isolated reports of jaundice, cholestatic hepatitis, and hepatitis. In most cases available information is incomplete.

OVERDOSAGE

Signs and symptoms of overdosage may be absent or mild (e.g. headache, nausea, confusion); but adverse cardiac events including cardiac arrest, ventricular arrhythmias including torsades de pointes and QT prolongation have been reported at overdoses of 360 mg or more and occur more frequently at doses in excess of 600 mg, and QTc prolongations of up to 30% have been observed at a dose of 300 mg b.i.d. Seizures and syncope have also been reported. USE OF DOSES IN EXCESS OF 60 MG B.I.D. IS NOT RECOMMENDED. (See WARNING BOX, CLINICAL PHARMACOLOGY, and ADVERSE REACTIONS.)

In overdose cases where ventricular arrhythmias are associated with significant QTc prolongation, treatment with antiarrhythmics known to prolong QTc intervals is not recommended.

Therefore, in cases of overdosage, cardiac monitoring for at least 24 hours is recommended and for as long as QTc is prolonged, along with standard measures to remove any unabsorbed drug. Limited experience with the use of hemoperfusion (N = 1) or hemodialysis (N = 3) was not successful in completely removing the acid metabolite of terfenadine from the blood.

Treatment of the signs and symptoms of overdosage should be symptomatic and supportive after the acute stage.

Oral LD$_{50}$ values for terfenadine were greater than 5000 mg/kg in mature mice and rats. The oral LD$_{50}$ was 438 mg/kg in newborn rats.

DOSAGE AND ADMINISTRATION

One tablet (60 mg) twice daily for adults and children 12 years and older. USE OF DOSES IN EXCESS OF 60 MG B.I.D. IS NOT RECOMMENDED BECAUSE OF THE INCREASED POTENTIAL FOR QT INTERVAL PROLONGATION AND ADVERSE CARDIAC EVENTS. (See WARNING BOX.) USE OF TERFENADINE IN PATIENTS WITH SIGNIFICANT HEPATIC DYSFUNCTION AND IN PATIENTS TAKING KETOCONAZOLE, ITRACONAZOLE, CLARITHROMYCIN, ERYTHROMYCIN, OR TROLEANDOMYCIN IS CONTRAINDICATED. (See CONTRAINDICATIONS, WARNINGS, and PRECAUTIONS: Drug Interactions.)

HOW SUPPLIED

NDC 0068-0723-61
  60 mg tablets in bottles of 100.
NDC 0068-0723-65
  60 mg tablets in bottles of 500.

Tablets are round, white, and debossed "SELDANE". Store tablets at controlled room temperature (59-86°F) (15-30°C). Protect from exposure to temperatures above 104°F (40°C) and moisture.

Prescribing Information as of January 1993

Merrell Dow Pharmaceuticals Inc.
Subsidiary of Marion Merrell Dow Inc.
Kansas City, MO 64114

U.S. Patents 3,878,217; 4,254,129.
Other patent applications pending.

selp0193c

Prescribing Information as of January 1993

SELDANE-D®

(terfenadine and pseudoephedrine hydrochloride) Extended-Release Tablets

WARNING BOX
QT INTERVAL PROLONGATION/VENTRICULAR ARRHYTHMIA

RARE CASES OF SERIOUS CARDIOVASCULAR ADVERSE EVENTS, INCLUDING DEATH, CARDIAC ARREST, TORSADES DE POINTES, AND OTHER VENTRICULAR ARRHYTHMIAS, HAVE BEEN OBSERVED IN THE FOLLOWING CLINICAL SETTINGS, FREQUENTLY IN ASSOCIATION WITH INCREASED TERFENADINE LEVELS WHICH LEAD TO ELECTROCARDIOGRAPHIC QT PROLONGATION:

1. **CONCOMITANT ADMINISTRATION OF KETOCONAZOLE (NIZORAL) OR ITRACONAZOLE (SPORANOX)**
2. **OVERDOSE, INCLUDING SINGLE TERFENADINE DOSES AS LOW AS 360 MG**
3. **CONCOMITANT ADMINISTRATION OF CLARITHROMYCIN, ERYTHROMYCIN, OR TROLEANDOMYCIN**
4. **SIGNIFICANT HEPATIC DYSFUNCTION**

TERFENADINE IS CONTRAINDICATED IN PATIENTS TAKING KETOCONAZOLE, ITRACONAZOLE, ERYTHROMYCIN, CLARITHROMYCIN, OR TROLEANDOMYCIN, AND IN PATIENTS WITH SIGNIFICANT HEPATIC DYSFUNCTION.

DO NOT EXCEED RECOMMENDED DOSE.

IN SOME CASES, SEVERE ARRHYTHMIAS HAVE BEEN PRECEDED BY EPISODES OF SYNCOPE. SYNCOPE IN PATIENTS RECEIVING TERFENADINE SHOULD LEAD TO DISCONTINUATION OF TREATMENT AND FULL EVALUATION OF POTENTIAL ARRHYTHMIAS.

(See CONTRAINDICATIONS, WARNINGS, CLINICAL PHARMACOLOGY, AND PRECAUTIONS: DRUG INTERACTIONS.)

DESCRIPTION

SELDANE-D (terfenadine and pseudoephedrine hydrochloride) Extended-Release Tablets are available for oral administration.

Each tablet contains 60 mg terfenadine and 10 mg of pseudoephedrine hydrochloride in an outer press-coat for immediate release and 110 mg pseudoephedrine hydrochloride in an extended-release core. Tablets also contain, as inactive ingredients: colloidal silicon dioxide, ethylcellulose, glycerin, hydroxypropyl cellulose, hydroxypropyl methylcellulose 2208, hydroxypropyl methylcellulose 2910, lactose, magnesium stearate, microcrystalline cellulose, polysorbate 80, precipitated calcium carbonate, pregelatinized corn starch, sodium lauryl sulfate, sodium starch glycolate, talc, titanium dioxide, and zinc stearate.

Terfenadine is a histamine H_1-receptor antagonist with the chemical name α-[4-(1,1-Dimethylethyl)phenyl]-4-(hydroxydiphenylmethyl)-1-piperidinebutanol (±). It has the following structure:

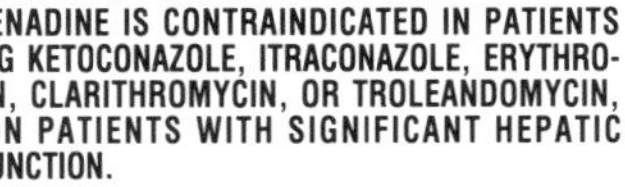

The molecular weight is 471.68. The molecular formula is $C_{32}H_{41}NO_2$.

Terfenadine occurs as a white to off-white crystalline powder. It is freely soluble in chloroform, soluble in ethanol, and very slightly soluble in water.

Pseudoephedrine hydrochloride is an adrenergic (vasoconstrictor) agent with the chemical name [S-(R*,R*)]-α-[1-(methylamino)ethyl]-benzenemethanol hydrochloride. It has the following chemical structure:

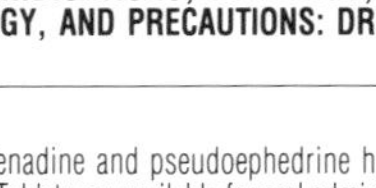

The molecular weight is 201.70. The molecular formula is $C_{10}H_{15}NO \bullet HCl$.

Pseudoephedrine hydrochloride occurs as fine, white to off-white crystals or powder, having a faint characteristic odor. It is very soluble in water, freely soluble in alcohol, and sparingly soluble in chloroform.

CLINICAL PHARMACOLOGY

Terfenadine, a histamine H_1-receptor antagonist, is chemically distinct from other antihistamines.

Histamine skin wheal studies have shown that terfenadine in single and repeated doses of 60 mg in 64 subjects has an antihistaminic effect beginning at 1-2 hours, reaching its maximum at 3-4 hours, and lasting in excess of 12 hours. The correlation between response on skin wheal testing and clinical efficacy is unclear.

The four best controlled and largest clinical trials of SELDANE each lasted 7 days and involved about 1,000 total patients in comparisons of SELDANE (60 mg b.i.d.) with an active drug (chlorpheniramine, 4 mg t.i.d.; dexchlorpheniramine, 2 mg t.i.d.; or clemastine 1 mg b.i.d.). About 50-70% of SELDANE or other antihistamine recipients had moderate to complete relief of symptoms, compared with 30-50% of placebo recipients. The frequency of drowsiness with SELDANE was similar to the frequency with placebo and less than with other antihistamines. In studies which included 52 subjects in whom EEG assessments were made, no depressant effects have been observed. SELDANE-D has not been studied for effectiveness in relieving the symptoms of the common cold.

Animal studies have demonstrated that terfenadine is a histamine H_1-receptor antagonist. In these animal studies, no sedative or anticholinergic effects were observed at effective antihistaminic doses. Radioactive disposition and autoradiographic studies in rats and radioligand binding studies with guinea pig brain H_1-receptors indicate that, at effective antihistamine doses, neither terfenadine nor its metabolites penetrate the blood brain barrier well.

On the basis of a mass balance study using ^{14}C labeled terfenadine the oral absorption of terfenadine was estimated to be at least 70%. Terfenadine itself undergoes extensive (99%) first pass metabolism to two primary metabolites, an active acid metabolite and an inactive dealkylated metabolite. Therefore, systemic availability of terfenadine is low under normal conditions, and parent terfenadine is not normally detectable in plasma at levels >10 ng/mL. Although in rare cases there was measurable plasma terfenadine in apparently normal individuals without identifiable risk factors, the implications of this finding with respect to the variability of terfenadine metabolism in the normal population cannot be assessed without further study. Further studies of terfenadine metabolism in the general population are pending. From information gained in the ^{14}C study it appears that approximately forty percent of the total dose is eliminated renally (40% as acid metabolite, 30% dealkyl metabolite, and 30% minor unidentified metabolites). Sixty percent of the dose is eliminated in the feces (50% as the acid metabolite, 2% unchanged terfenadine, and the remainder as minor unidentified metabolites). Studies investigating the effect of hepatic and renal insufficiency on the metabolism and excretion of terfenadine are incomplete. Preliminary information indicates that in cases of hepatic impairment, significant concentrations of unchanged terfenadine can be detected with the rate of acid metabolite formation being decreased. A single-dose study in patients with hepatic impairment revealed increased parent terfenadine and impaired metabolism, suggesting that additional drug accumulation may occur after repetitive dosing in such patients. Terfenadine is contraindicated for use in patients with significant hepatic dysfunction. (See CONTRAINDICATIONS and WARNINGS.) In subjects with normal hepatic function unchanged terfenadine plasma concentrations have not been detected. **Elevated levels of parent terfenadine, whether due to significant hepatic dysfunction, concomitant medications, or overdose, have been associated with QT interval prolongation and serious cardiac adverse events.** (See CONTRAINDICATIONS and WARNINGS.) In controlled clinical trials in otherwise normal patients with rhinitis, small increases in QTc interval were observed at doses of 60 mg b.i.d. In studies at 300 mg b.i.d. a mean increase in QTc of 10% (range −4% to +30%) (mean increase of 46 msec) was observed.

Data have been reported demonstrating that compared to young subjects, elderly subjects experience a 25% reduction in clearance of the acid metabolite after single-dose oral administration of 120 mg. Further studies are necessary to fully characterize pharmacokinetics in the elderly.

In vitro studies demonstrate that terfenadine is extensively (97%) bound to human serum protein while the acid metabolite is approximately 70% bound to human serum protein. Based on data gathered from in vitro models of antihistaminic activity, the acid metabolite of terfenadine has approximately 30% of the H_1-blocking activity of terfenadine. The relative contribution of terfenadine and the acid metabolite to the pharmacodynamic effects have not been clearly defined. Since unchanged terfenadine is usually not detected in plasma and active acid metabolite concentrations are relatively high, the acid metabolite may be the entity responsible for the majority of efficacy after oral administration of terfenadine.

In a study involving the administration of a single 60 mg terfenadine tablet to 24 subjects, mean peak plasma levels of the acid metabolite were 263 ng/mL (range 133-423 ng/mL) and occurred approximately 2.5 hours after dosing. Plasma concentrations of unchanged terfenadine were not detected. The elimination profile of the acid metabolite was biphasic in nature with an initial mean plasma half-life of 3.5 hours followed by a mean plasma half-life of 6 hours. Ninety percent of the plasma level time curve was associated with these half-lives. Although the elimination profile is somewhat complex, the effective pharmacokinetic half-life can be estimated at approximately 8.5 hours. However, receptor binding and pharmacologic effects, both therapeutic and adverse, may persist well beyond that time.

Pseudoephedrine is an orally active sympathomimetic amine and exerts a decongestant action on the nasal mucosa. It is recognized as an effective agent for the relief of nasal congestion due to allergic rhinitis. Pseudoephedrine produces peripheral effects similar to those of epinephrine and central effects similar to, but less intense than, amphetamines. It has the potential for excitatory side effects. At the recommended oral dose it has little or no pressor effect in normotensive adults. The serum half-life of pseudoephedrine is approximately 4 to 6 hours. The serum half-life is decreased with increased excretion of drug at urine pH lower than 6 and may be increased with decreased excretion at urine pH higher than 8.

Ingestion of food was found not to affect the absorption of pseudoephedrine from SELDANE-D. The effect of food on the absorption of terfenadine from SELDANE-D is not known; however, plasma levels of the active metabolite do not appear to be affected by food administered with SELDANE-D.

A bioavailability study comparing SELDANE-D to immediate-release terfenadine and immediate-release pseudoephedrine showed that pseudoephedrine is slowly released from SELDANE-D to permit twice daily dosage.

INDICATIONS AND USAGE

SELDANE-D is indicated for the relief of symptoms associated with seasonal allergic rhinitis such as sneezing, rhinorrhea, pruritus, lacrimation, and nasal congestion. It should be administered when both the antihistaminic properties of SELDANE (terfenadine) and the nasal decongestant activity of pseudoephedrine hydrochloride are desired (see CLINICAL PHARMACOLOGY).

SELDANE-D has not been studied for effectiveness in relieving the symptoms of the common cold.

CONTRAINDICATIONS

CONCOMITANT ADMINISTRATION OF SELDANE-D WITH KETOCONAZOLE (NIZORAL) OR ITRACONAZOLE (SPORANOX) IS CONTRAINDICATED. SELDANE-D IS ALSO CONTRAINDICATED IN PATIENTS WITH DISEASE STATES OR OTHER CONCOMITANT MEDICATIONS KNOWN TO IMPAIR ITS METABOLISM, INCLUDING SIGNIFICANT HEPATIC DYSFUNCTION, AND CONCURRENT USE OF CLARITHROMYCIN, ERYTHROMYCIN, OR TROLEANDOMYCIN. QT PROLONGATION HAS BEEN DEMONSTRATED IN SOME PATIENTS TAKING TERFENADINE IN THESE SETTINGS, AND RARE CASES OF SERIOUS CARDIOVASCULAR EVENTS, INCLUDING DEATH, CARDIAC ARREST, AND TORSADES DE POINTES, HAVE BEEN REPORTED IN THESE PATIENT POPULATIONS. (See WARNINGS and PRECAUTIONS: Drug Interactions.)

SELDANE-D is contraindicated in nursing mothers, patients with severe hypertension or severe coronary artery disease, patients receiving monoamine oxidase (MAO) inhibitor therapy, and in patients with a known hypersensitivity to any of its ingredients (see DESCRIPTION section).

WARNINGS

Terfenadine undergoes extensive metabolism in the liver by a specific cytochrome P-450 isoenzyme. This metabolic pathway may be impaired in patients with hepatic dysfunction (alcoholic cirrhosis, hepatitis) or who are taking drugs such as ketoconazole, itraconazole, or clarithromycin, erythromycin, or troleandomycin (macrolide antibiotics), or other potent inhibitors of this isoenzyme. Interference with this metabolism can lead to elevated terfenadine plasma levels associated with QT prolongation and increased risk of ventricular tachyarrhythmias (such as torsades de pointes, ventricular tachycardia, and ventricular fibrillation) at the recommended dose. SELDANE-D is contraindicated for use by patients with these conditions (see WARNING BOX, CONTRAINDICATIONS, and PRECAUTIONS: Drug Interactions).

Other patients who may be at risk for these adverse cardiovascular events include patients who may experience new or increased QT prolongation while receiving certain drugs or having conditions which lead to QT prolongation. These include patients taking certain antiarrhythmics, bepridil, certain psychotropics, probucol, or astemizole; patients with electrolyte abnormalities such as hypokalemia or hypomagnesemia, or taking diuretics with potential for inducing electrolyte abnormalities; and patients with congenital QT syndrome. SELDANE-D is not recommended for use by patients with these conditions.

The relationship of underlying cardiac disease to the development of ventricular tachyarrhythmias while on SELDANE-D therapy is unclear; nonetheless, SELDANE-D should also be used with caution in these patients.

Sympathomimetic amines should be used judiciously and sparingly in patients with hypertension, diabetes mellitus, ischemic heart disease, increased intraocular pressure, hyperthyroidism, or prostatic hypertrophy (see CONTRAINDICATIONS). Sympathomimetic amines may produce CNS stimulation with convulsions or cardiovascular collapse with accompanying hypotension.

Use in Elderly

The elderly are more likely to have adverse reactions to sympathomimetic amines.

PRECAUTIONS

General

SELDANE-D should be used with caution in patients with diabetes, hypertension, cardiovascular disease, and hyperreactivity to ephedrine.

Information for Patients
Patients taking SELDANE-D should receive the following information and instructions. Patients should be advised to take SELDANE-D only as needed and NOT TO EXCEED THE PRESCRIBED DOSE. Patients should be questioned about use of any other prescription or over-the-counter medication, and should be cautioned regarding the potential for life-threatening arrhythmias with concurrent use of ketoconazole, itraconazole, clarithromycin, erythromycin, or troleandomycin. Patients should be advised to consult the physician before concurrent use of other medications with terfenadine. Patients should be questioned about pregnancy or lactation before starting SELDANE-D therapy, since the drug is contraindicated in nursing women and should be used in pregnancy only if the potential benefit justifies the potential risk to the fetus. Patients should be directed to swallow the tablet whole. Patients should also be instructed to store this medication in a tightly closed container in a cool, dry place, away from heat, moisture, or direct sunlight, and away from children.

Drug Interactions (see CONTRAINDICATIONS)
Monoamine oxidase (MAO) inhibitors and beta-adrenergic agonists increase the effect of sympathomimetic amines. Sympathomimetic amines may reduce the antihypertensive effects of methyldopa, mecamylamine, and reserpine. MAO inhibitors may prolong and intensify the effects of antihistamines.
Care should be taken in the administration of SELDANE-D concomitantly with other sympathomimetic amines because combined effects on the cardiovascular system may be harmful to the patient.

Ketoconazole
Spontaneous adverse reaction reports of patients taking concomitant ketoconazole with recommended doses of terfenadine demonstrate QT interval prolongation and rare serious cardiac events, e.g. death, cardiac arrest, and ventricular arrhythmia including torsades de pointes. Pharmacokinetic data indicate that ketoconazole markedly inhibits the metabolism of terfenadine, resulting in elevated plasma terfenadine levels. Presence of unchanged terfenadine is associated with statistically significant prolongation of the QT and QTc intervals. **Concomitant administration of ketoconazole and SELDANE-D is contraindicated** (see CONTRAINDICATIONS, WARNINGS, and ADVERSE REACTIONS).

Itraconazole
Torsades de pointes and elevated parent terfenadine levels have been reported during concomitant use of terfenadine and itraconazole in clinical trials of itraconazole and from foreign post-marketing sources. One death has also been reported from foreign post-marketing sources. **Concomitant administration of itraconazole and SELDANE-D is contraindicated** (see CONTRAINDICATIONS, WARNINGS, and ADVERSE REACTIONS).
Due to the chemical similarity of other azole-type antifungal agents (including fluconazole, metronidazole, and miconazole) to ketoconazole and itraconazole, concomitant use of these products with SELDANE-D is not recommended pending full examination of potential interactions.

Macrolides
Clinical drug interactions studies indicate that erythromycin and clarithromycin can exert an effect on terfenadine metabolism by a mechanism which may be similar to that of ketoconazole, but to a lesser extent. Although erythromycin measurably decreases the clearance of the terfenadine acid metabolite, its influence on terfenadine plasma levels is still under investigation. A few spontaneous accounts of QT interval prolongation with ventricular arrhythmia including torsades de pointes have been reported in patients receiving erythromycin and troleandomycin.
Concomitant administration of SELDANE-D with clarithromycin, erythromycin, or troleandomycin is contraindicated (see CONTRAINDICATIONS, WARNINGS, and ADVERSE REACTIONS). Pending full characterization of potential interactions, concomitant administration of SELDANE-D with other macrolide antibiotics, including azithromycin is not recommended. Studies to evaluate potential interaction of terfenadine with azithromycin are in progress.

Carcinogenesis, Mutagenesis, Impairment of Fertility
No studies have been conducted to evaluate the carcinogenic potential of SELDANE-D.
Oral doses of terfenadine, corresponding to 63 times the recommended human daily dose, in mice for 18 months or in rats for 24 months, revealed no evidence of tumorigenicity. Microbial and micronucleus test assays with terfenadine have revealed no evidence of mutagenesis.
Reproduction and fertility studies with terfenadine in rats showed no effects on male or female fertility at oral doses of up to 21 times the human daily dose. At 63 times the human daily dose there was a small but significant reduction in implants and at 125 times the human daily dose reduced implants and increased post-implantation losses were observed, which were judged to be secondary to maternal toxicity. Animal reproduction studies have not been carried out with pseudoephedrine.

Pregnancy Category C
The combination of terfenadine and pseudoephedrine hydrochloride (in a ratio of 1:2 by weight) has been shown to produce reduced fetal weight in rats and rabbits at 42 times the human dose, and delayed ossification with wavy ribs in a few fetuses when given to rats at a dose of 63 times the human daily dose. There are no adequate and well-controlled studies in pregnant women. SELDANE-D should be used during pregnancy only if the potential benefit justifies the potential risk to the fetus.

Nursing Mothers (see CONTRAINDICATIONS)
Terfenadine has caused decreased pup weight gain and survival in rats given doses 63 times and 125 times the human daily dose throughout pregnancy and lactation.

Pediatric Use
Safety and effectiveness of SELDANE-D in children below the age of 12 years have not been established.

ADVERSE REACTIONS

Cardiovascular Adverse Events
With terfenadine, rare reports of severe cardiovascular adverse effects have been received which include ventricular tachyarrhythmias (torsades de pointes, ventricular tachycardia, ventricular fibrillation, and cardiac arrest), hypotension, palpitations, syncope, and dizziness. Rare reports of deaths resulting from ventricular tachyarrhythmias have been received (see CONTRAINDICATIONS, WARNINGS, and PRECAUTIONS: Drug Interactions). Hypotension, palpitations, syncope, and dizziness could reflect undetected ventricular arrhythmia. IN SOME PATIENTS, DEATH, CARDIAC ARREST, OR TORSADES DE POINTES HAVE BEEN PRECEDED BY EPISODES OF SYNCOPE. (See WARNING BOX.) Rare reports of serious cardiovascular adverse events have been received, some involving QT prolongation and torsades de pointes, in apparently normal individuals without identifiable risk factors; there is not conclusive evidence of a causal relationship of these events with terfenadine. Although in rare cases there was measurable plasma terfenadine, the implications of this finding with respect to the variability of terfenadine metabolism in the normal population cannot be assessed without further study. In controlled clinical trials in otherwise normal patients with rhinitis, small increases in QTc interval were observed at doses of 60 mg b.i.d. In studies at 300 mg b.i.d. a mean increase in QTc of 10% (range −4% to +30%) (mean increase of 46 msec) was observed.

General Adverse Events
In double-blind, parallel, controlled studies in over 300 patients in which SELDANE-D was compared to extended-release pseudoephedrine, adverse reactions reported for greater than 1% of the patients receiving SELDANE-D were not clinically different from those reported for patients receiving pseudoephedrine (see Table below).

Frequently (>1%) Reported Adverse Events for SELDANE-D in Double-blind, Parallel, Controlled Clinical Trials*

	Percent of Patients Reporting		
Adverse Event	SELDANE-D (N=374)	Pseudo-ephedrine (N=287)	Placebo (N=193)
Central Nervous System			
Insomnia	25.9	26.8	6.2
Headache	17.4	17.1	22.3
Drowsiness/Sedation	7.2	4.9	11.4
Nervousness	6.7	8.4	1.6
Anorexia	3.7	3.8	0.0
Fatigue	2.1	1.4	2.1
Restlessness	2.1	1.0	0.0
Irritability	1.1	0.0	1.0
Disorientation	1.1	0.0	0.5
Increased Energy	1.1	0.0	0.0
Hyperkinesia	1.1	1.0	0.0
Autonomic			
Dry Mouth/Nose/Throat	21.7	21.3	11.4
Blurring of Vision	1.1	0.3	0.5
Gastrointestinal			
Nausea	4.5	6.6	5.2
Skin			
Rash	1.1	0.0	0.0
Cardiovascular			
Palpitations	2.4	3.8	0.5
Allergy Symptoms			
Sore Throat	1.9	1.7	1.0
Cough	1.6	0.3	1.0
Other			
Infection, Upper Respiratory	1.3	2.4	0.5
Taste Alterations	1.1	1.0	1.0

*SELDANE-D B.I.D., pseudoephedrine 120 mg B.I.D.

Pseudoephedrine may cause ephedrine-like reactions such as tachycardia, palpitations, headache, dizziness, or nausea. Sympathomimetic drugs have also been associated with certain untoward reactions including fear, anxiety, tenseness, restlessness, tremor, weakness, pallor, respiratory difficulty, dysuria, insomnia, hallucinations, convulsions, CNS depression, arrhythmias, and cardiovascular collapse with hypotension.

In controlled clinical trials with terfenadine, using the recommended daily dose of 60 mg b.i.d., the incidence of adverse events in patients receiving terfenadine was similar to that reported in patients receiving placebo. These effects included:
Central Nervous System: Drowsiness, headache, fatigue, dizziness, nervousness, weakness, appetite increase
Gastrointestinal System: Abdominal distress, nausea, vomiting, change in bowel habits
Eye, Ear, Nose and Throat:: Dry mouth/nose/throat, cough, sore throat, epistaxis
Skin: Eruption (including rash and urticaria) or itching
Also reported spontaneously during the marketing of terfenadine were: alopecia (hair loss or thinning), anaphylaxis, angioedema, bronchospasm, confusion, depression, galactorrhea, insomnia, menstrual disorders (including dysmenorrhea), musculoskeletal symptoms, nightmares, paresthesia, photosensitivity, rapid flare of psoriasis, seizures, sinus tachycardia, sweating, thrombocytopenia, tremor, urinary frequency, and visual disturbances.
Also in clinical trials, several instances of mild or, in one case, moderate transaminase elevations were seen in patients receiving terfenadine. Mild elevations were also seen in placebo treated patients. Marketing experiences include isolated reports of jaundice, cholestatic hepatitis, and hepatitis. In most cases available information is incomplete.

OVERDOSAGE
Acute overdosage with SELDANE-D tablets may produce clinical signs of CNS stimulation or depression and various cardiovascular effects, including cardiac collapse and death. Sympathomimetic amines should be used with great caution in the presence of pseudoephedrine. Patients with signs of stimulation should be treated conservatively.
Adverse cardiac events including cardiac arrest, ventricular arrhythmias including torsades de pointes and QT prolongation have been reported at overdoses of 360 mg or more of terfenadine and occur more frequently at doses in excess of 600 mg, and QTc prolongations of up to 30% have been observed at a dose of 300 mg b.i.d. Seizures and syncope have also been reported. USE OF DOSES IN EXCESS OF ONE TABLET B.I.D. IS NOT RECOMMENDED. (See WARNING BOX, CLINICAL PHARMACOLOGY, and ADVERSE REACTIONS.)
In overdose cases where ventricular arrhythmias are associated with significant QTc prolongation, treatment with antiarrhythmics known to prolong QTc intervals is not recommended.
Therefore, in cases of overdosage, cardiac monitoring for at least 24 hours is recommended and for as long as QTc is prolonged, along with standard measures to remove any unabsorbed drug. Limited experience with the use of hemoperfusion (N = 1) and hemodialysis (N = 3) was not successful in completely removing the acid metabolite of terfenadine from the blood.
Oral LD_{50} values for terfenadine were greater than 5000 mg/kg in mature mice and rats. The oral LD_{50} was 438 mg/kg in newborn rats. The LD_{50} of pseudoephedrine hydrochloride alone in male and female rats was 1674 mg/kg, while the LD_{50} of pseudoephedrine hydrochloride administered with terfenadine was 3017 mg/kg.

DOSAGE AND ADMINISTRATION
Adults and children 12 years and older: one tablet swallowed whole, morning and night.
USE OF DOSES IN EXCESS OF ONE TABLET B.I.D. IS NOT RECOMMENDED BECAUSE OF THE INCREASED POTENTIAL FOR QT INTERVAL PROLONGATION AND ADVERSE CARDIAC EVENTS. (See WARNING BOX.) USE OF SELDANE-D IN PATIENTS WITH SIGNIFICANT HEPATIC DYSFUNCTION AND IN PATIENTS TAKING KETOCONAZOLE, ITRACONAZOLE, CLARITHROMYCIN, ERYTHROMYCIN, OR TROLEANDOMYCIN IS CONTRAINDICATED. (See CONTRAINDICATIONS, WARNINGS, and PRECAUTIONS: Drug Interactions.)

HOW SUPPLIED
SELDANE-D Tablets containing 60 mg of terfenadine and 10 mg of pseudoephedrine hydrochloride in an outer press-coat for immediate release and 110 mg of pseudoephedrine hydrochloride in an extended-release core are supplied as follows:
NDC 0068-0722-61: Bottles of 100 tablets.
Tablets are white to off-white, biconvex capsule-shaped; debossed "SELDANE-D". Store at controlled room temperature (59-86°F) (15-30°C). Protect from moisture.

Prescribing Information as of January 1993

Merrell Dow Pharmaceuticals Inc.
Subsidiary of Marion Merrell Dow Inc.
Kansas City, MO 64114

U.S. Patents 3,878,217; 4,929,605; 4,996,061; 4,254,129.

sedp0193c

Prescribing Information as of October 1992

CARAFATE® Tablets
(sucralfate)

DESCRIPTION
CARAFATE (sucralfate) is an α-D-glucopyranoside, β-D-fructofuranosyl-, octakis-(hydrogen sulfate), aluminum complex.

$$R = SO_3[Al_2 (OH)_5 \cdot (H_2O)_2]$$

Tablets for oral administration contain 1 gm of sucralfate.
Also contain: D&C Red # 30 Lake, FD&C Blue # 1 Lake, magnesium stearate, microcrystalline cellulose, and starch.
Therapeutic category: antiulcer.

CLINICAL PHARMACOLOGY
Sucralfate is only minimally absorbed from the gastrointestinal tract. The small amounts of the sulfated disaccharide that are absorbed are excreted primarily in the urine.
Although the mechanism of sucralfate's ability to accelerate healing of duodenal ulcers remains to be fully defined, it is known that it exerts its effect through a local, rather than systemic, action. The following observations also appear pertinent:

1. Studies in human subjects and with animal models of ulcer disease have shown that sucralfate forms an ulcer-adherent complex with proteinaceous exudate at the ulcer site.
2. In vitro, a sucralfate-albumin film provides a barrier to diffusion of hydrogen ions.
3. In human subjects, sucralfate given in doses recommended for ulcer therapy inhibits pepsin activity in gastric juice by 32%.
4. In vitro, sucralfate adsorbs bile salts.

These observations suggest that sucralfate's antiulcer activity is the result of formation of an ulcer-adherent complex that covers the ulcer site and protects it against further attack by acid, pepsin, and bile salts. There are approximately 14-16 mEq of acid-neutralizing capacity per 1-gm dose of sucralfate.

CLINICAL TRIALS
Acute Duodenal Ulcer
Over 600 patients have participated in well-controlled clinical trials worldwide. Multicenter trials conducted in the United States, both of them placebo-controlled studies with endoscopic evaluation at 2 and 4 weeks, showed:

STUDY 1

Treatment Groups	Ulcer Healing/No. Patients	
	2 wk	4 wk (Overall)
Sucralfate	37/105 (35.2%)	82/109 (75.2%)
Placebo	26/106 (24.5%)	68/107 (63.6%)

STUDY 2

Treatment Groups	Ulcer Healing/No. Patients	
	2 wk	4 wk (Overall)
Sucralfate	8/24 (33%)	22/24 (92%)
Placebo	4/31 (13%)	18/31 (58%)

The sucralfate-placebo differences were statistically significant in both studies at 4 weeks but not at 2 weeks. The poorer result in the first study may have occurred because sucralfate was given 2 hours after meals and at bedtime rather than 1 hour before meals and at bedtime, the regimen used in international studies and in the second United States study. In addition, in the first study liquid antacid was utilized as needed, whereas in the second study antacid tablets were used.

Maintenance Therapy After Healing of Duodenal Ulcer
Two double-blind randomized placebo-controlled U.S. multicenter trials have demonstrated that sucralfate (1 gm bid) is effective as maintenance therapy following healing of duodenal ulcers.
In one study, endoscopies were performed monthly for 4 months. Of the 254 patients who enrolled, 239 were analyzed in the intention-to-treat life table analysis presented below.

Duodenal Ulcer Recurrence Rate (%)					
Months of Therapy					
Drug	N	1	2	3	4
CARAFATE	122	20*	30*	38**	42**
Placebo	117	33	46	55	63

*p<0.05, **p<0.01
Prn antacids were not permitted in this study.

In the other study, scheduled endoscopies were performed at 6 and 12 months, but for cause endoscopies were permitted as symptoms dictated. Median symptom scores between the sucralfate and placebo groups were not significantly different. A life table intention-to-treat analysis for the 94 patients enrolled in the trial had the following results:

Duodenal Ulcer Recurrence Rate (%)			
Drug	N	6 months	12 months
CARAFATE	48	19*	27*
Placebo	46	54	65

*p<0.002
Prn antacids were permitted in this study.
Data from placebo-controlled studies longer than 1 year are not available.

INDICATIONS AND USAGE
CARAFATE® (sucralfate) is indicated in:
- Short-term treatment (up to 8 weeks) of active duodenal ulcer. While healing with sucralfate may occur during the first week or two, treatment should be continued for 4 to 8 weeks unless healing has been demonstrated by x-ray or endoscopic examination.
- Maintenance therapy for duodenal ulcer patients at reduced dosage after healing of acute ulcers.

CONTRAINDICATIONS
There are no known contraindications to the use of sucralfate.

PRECAUTIONS
Duodenal ulcer is a chronic, recurrent disease. While short-term treatment with sucralfate can result in complete healing of the ulcer, a successful course of treatment with sucralfate should not be expected to alter the posthealing frequency or severity of duodenal ulceration.

Special Populations: Chronic Renal Failure and Dialysis Patients
When sucralfate is administered orally, small amounts of aluminum are absorbed from the gastrointestinal tract. Concomitant use of sucralfate with other products that contain aluminum, such as aluminum-containing antacids, may increase the total body burden of aluminum. Patients with normal renal function receiving the recommended doses of sucralfate and aluminum-containing products adequately excrete aluminum in the urine. Patients with chronic renal failure or those receiving dialysis have impaired excretion of absorbed aluminum. In addition, aluminum does not cross dialysis membranes because it is bound to albumin and transferrin plasma proteins. Aluminum accumulation and toxicity (aluminum osteodystrophy, osteomalacia, encephalopathy) have been described in patients with renal impairment. Sucralfate should be used with caution in patients with chronic renal failure.

Drug Interactions
Some studies have shown that simultaneous sucralfate administration in healthy volunteers reduced the extent of absorption (bioavailability) of single doses of the following drugs: cimetidine, ciprofloxacin, digoxin, ketoconazole, norfloxacin, phenytoin, ranitidine, tetracycline, and theophylline. Subtherapeutic prothrombin times with concomitant warfarin and sucralfate therapy have been reported in spontaneous and published case reports. However, two clinical studies have demonstrated no change in either serum warfarin concentration or prothrombin time with the addition of sucralfate to chronic warfarin therapy.
The mechanism of these interactions appears to be nonsystemic in nature, presumably resulting from sucralfate binding to the concomitant agent in the gastrointestinal tract. In all cases studied to date (cimetidine, ciprofloxacin, digoxin, ranitidine, and warfarin), dosing the concomitant medication 2 hours before sucralfate eliminated the interaction. Because of the potential of CARAFATE to alter the absorption of some drugs, CARAFATE should be administered separately from other drugs when alterations in bioavailability are felt to be critical. In these cases, patients should be monitored appropriately.

Carcinogenesis, Mutagenesis, Impairment of Fertility
Chronic oral toxicity studies of 24 months' duration were conducted in mice and rats at doses up to 1 gm/kg (12 times the human dose). There was no evidence of drug-related tumorigenicity. A reproduction study in rats at doses up to 38 times the human dose did not reveal any indication of fertility impairment. Mutagenicity studies were not conducted.

Pregnancy
Teratogenic effects. Pregnancy Category B. Teratogenicity studies have been performed in mice, rats, and rabbits at doses up to 50 times the human dose and have revealed no evidence of harm to the fetus due to sucralfate. There are, however, no adequate and well-controlled studies in pregnant women. Because animal reproduction studies are not always predictive of human response, this drug should be used during pregnancy only if clearly needed.

Nursing Mothers
It is not known whether this drug is excreted in human milk. Because many drugs are excreted in human milk, caution should be exercised when sucralfate is administered to a nursing woman.

Pediatric Use
Safety and effectiveness in children have not been established.

ADVERSE REACTIONS
Adverse reactions to sucralfate in clinical trials were minor and only rarely led to discontinuation of the drug. In studies involving over 2700 patients treated with sucralfate tablets, adverse effects were reported in 129 (4.7%).
Constipation was the most frequent complaint (2%). Other adverse effects reported in less than 0.5% of the patients are listed below by body system:
Gastrointestinal: diarrhea, nausea, vomiting, gastric discomfort, indigestion, flatulence, dry mouth
Dermatological: pruritus, rash
Nervous System: dizziness, insomnia, sleepiness, vertigo
Other: back pain, headache
Postmarketing reports of hypersensitivity reactions, including urticaria (hives), angioedema, respiratory difficulty, and rhinitis have been received. However, a causal relationship has not been established.

OVERDOSAGE
There is no experience in humans with overdosage. Acute oral toxicity studies in animals, however, using doses up to 12 gm/kg body weight, could not find a lethal dose. Risks associated with overdosage should, therefore, be minimal.

DOSAGE AND ADMINISTRATION
Active Duodenal Ulcer: The recommended adult oral dosage for duodenal ulcer is 1 gm four times a day on an empty stomach.
Antacids may be prescribed as needed for relief of pain but should not be taken within one-half hour before or after sucralfate.
While healing with sucralfate may occur during the first week or two, treatment should be continued for 4 to 8 weeks unless healing has been demonstrated by x-ray or endoscopic examination.
Maintenance Therapy: The recommended adult oral dosage is 1 gm twice a day.

HOW SUPPLIED
CARAFATE (sucralfate) 1-gm tablets are supplied in bottles of 100 (NDC 0088-1712-47), 120 (NDC 0088-1712-53), and 500 (NDC 0088-1712-55) and in Unit Dose Identification Paks of 100 (NDC 0088-1712-49). Light pink scored oblong tablets are embossed with CARAFATE on one side and 1712 on the other.

Prescribing Information as of October 1992

Marion Merrell Dow Inc.
Kansas City, MO 64114

cafp1092c

Prescribing Information as of January 1992

NICODERM®
(nicotine transdermal system)

Systemic delivery of 21, 14, or 7 mg/day over 24 hours

DESCRIPTION

NICODERM is a transdermal system that provides systemic delivery of nicotine for 24 hours following its application to intact skin.

Nicotine is a tertiary amine composed of a pyridine and a pyrrolidine ring. It is a colorless to pale yellow, freely water-soluble, strongly alkaline, oily, volatile, hygroscopic liquid obtained from the tobacco plant. Nicotine has a characteristic pungent odor and turns brown on exposure to air or light. Of its two stereoisomers, S(-)-nicotine is the more active and is the more prevalent form in tobacco. The free alkaloid is absorbed rapidly through the skin and respiratory tract.

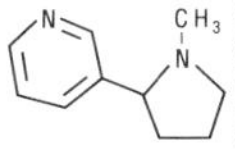

Chemical Name: S-3-(1-methyl-2-pyrrolidinyl) pyridine
Molecular Formula: $C_{10}H_{14}N_2$
Molecular Weight: 162.23
Ionization Constants: $pK_a1=7.84$, $pK_a2 = 3.04$
Octanol-Water Partition Coefficient: 15:1 at pH7

The NICODERM system is a multilayered rectangular film containing nicotine as the active agent. For the three doses the composition per unit area is identical. Proceeding from the visible surface toward the surface attached to the skin are (1) an occlusive backing (polyethylene/aluminum/polyester/ethylene-vinyl acetate copolymer); (2) a drug reservoir containing nicotine (in an ethylene-vinyl acetate copolymer matrix); (3) a rate-controlling membrane (polyethylene); (4) a polyisobutylene adhesive; and (5) a protective liner that covers the adhesive layer and must be removed before application to the skin.

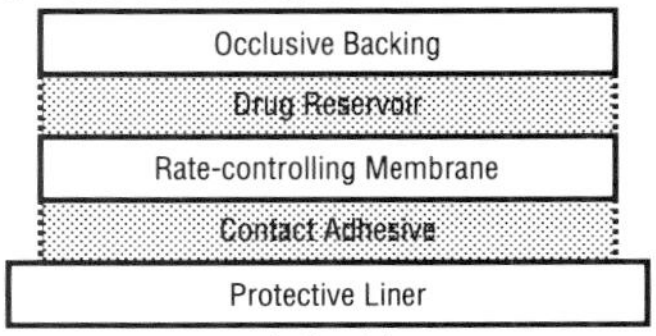

(not to scale)

Nicotine is the active ingredient; other components of the system are pharmacologically inactive.

The rate of delivery of nicotine to the patient from each system (40 μg/cm²-h) is proportional to the surface area. About 73% of the total amount of nicotine remains in the system 24 hours after application. NICODERM systems are labeled by the dose actually absorbed by the patient. The dose of nicotine absorbed from the NICODERM system represents 68% of the amount released in 24 hours. The other 32% (eg, 9 mg/day for the 21 mg/day system) volatizes from the edge of the system.

Dose Absorbed in 24 Hours (mg/day)	System Area (cm²)	Total Nicotine Content (mg)
21	22	114
14	15	78
7	7	36

CLINICAL PHARMACOLOGY

Pharmacologic Action

Nicotine, the chief alkaloid in tobacco products, binds stereoselectively to acetylcholine receptors at the autonomic ganglia, in the adrenal medulla, at neuromuscular junctions, and in the brain. Two types of central nervous system effects are believed to be the basis of nicotine's positively reinforcing properties. A stimulating effect, exerted mainly in the cortex via the locus ceruleus, produces increased alertness and cognitive performance. A "reward" effect via the "pleasure system" in the brain is exerted in the limbic system. At low doses the stimulant effects predominate, while at high doses the reward effects predominate. Intermittent intravenous administration of nicotine activates neurohormonal pathways, releasing acetylcholine, norepinephrine, dopamine, serotonin, vasopressin, beta-endorphin, growth hormone, and ACTH.

Pharmacodynamics

The cardiovascular effects of nicotine include peripheral vasoconstriction, tachycardia, and elevated blood pressure. Acute and chronic tolerance to nicotine develops from smoking tobacco or ingesting nicotine preparations. Acute tolerance (a reduction in response for a given dose) develops rapidly (less than 1 hour), but at distinct rates for different physiologic effects (skin temperature, heart rate, subjective effects). Withdrawal symptoms, such as cigarette craving, can be reduced in some individuals by plasma nicotine levels lower than those for smoking.

Withdrawal from nicotine in addicted individuals is characterized by craving, nervousness, restlessness, irritability, mood lability, anxiety, drowsiness, sleep disturbances, impaired concentration, increased appetite, minor somatic complaints (headache, myalgia, constipation, fatigue), and weight gain. Nicotine toxicity is characterized by nausea, abdominal pain, vomiting, diarrhea, diaphoresis, flushing, dizziness, disturbed hearing and vision, confusion, weakness, palpitations, altered respiration, and hypotension.

The cardiovascular effects of NICODERM 21 mg/day used continuously for 24 hours and smoking every 30 minutes during waking hours for 5 days were compared. Both regimens elevated heart rate (about 10 beats/min) and blood pressure (about 5 mm Hg) compared with an abstinence period, and these increases were similar between treatments throughout the 24-hour period, including during sleep.

The circadian pattern and release of plasma cortisol following 5 days of treatment with NICODERM 21 mg/day did not differ from that following 5 days of nicotine abstinence. Urinary excretion of norepinephrine, epinephrine, and dopamine was also similar for NICODERM 21 mg/day and abstinence.

Pharmacokinetics

Following application of the NICODERM system to the upper body or upper outer arm, approximately 68% of the nicotine released from the system enters the systemic circulation (eg, 21 mg/day for the highest dose of NICODERM). The remainder of the nicotine released from the system is lost via evaporation from the edge. All NICODERM systems are labeled by the actual amount of nicotine absorbed by the patient.

The volume of distribution following IV administration of nicotine is approximately 2 to 3 L/kg, and the half-life of nicotine ranges from 1 to 2 hours. The major eliminating organ is the liver, and average plasma clearance is about 1.2 L/min; the kidney and lung also metabolize nicotine. There is no significant skin metabolism of nicotine. More than 20 metabolites of nicotine have been identified, all of which are believed to be less active than the parent compound. The primary metabolite of nicotine in plasma, cotinine, has a half-life of 15 to 20 hours and concentrations that exceed nicotine by 10-fold.

Plasma protein binding of nicotine is <5%. Therefore, changes in nicotine binding from use of concomitant drugs or alterations of plasma proteins by disease states would not be expected to have significant consequences.

The primary urinary metabolites are cotinine (15% of the dose) and trans-3-hydroxycotinine (45% of the dose). About 10% of nicotine is excreted unchanged in the urine. As much as 30% may be excreted in the urine with high urine flow rates and urine acidification below pH 5.

After NICODERM application, plasma concentrations rise rapidly, plateau within 2 to 4 hours, and then slowly decline until the system is removed; after which they decline more rapidly.

The pharmacokinetic model that best fits the plasma nicotine concentrations from NICODERM systems is an open, two-compartment disposition model with a skin depot through which nicotine enters the central circulation compartment. Nicotine in the adhesive layer is absorbed into and then through the skin, causing the initial rapid rise in plasma concentrations. The nicotine from the reservoir is released slowly through the membrane with a release rate constant approximately 20 times smaller than the skin absorption rate constant, as demonstrated *in vitro* in cadaver skin flux studies and verified by pharmacokinetic trials. Therefore, the slow decline of plasma nicotine concentrations during 4 to 24 hours (see Figure) is determined primarily by the release of nicotine from the system.

Steady-State Plasma Nicotine Concentrations for Two Consecutive Applications of Nicoderm 21 mg/day (Mean ±2 SD)

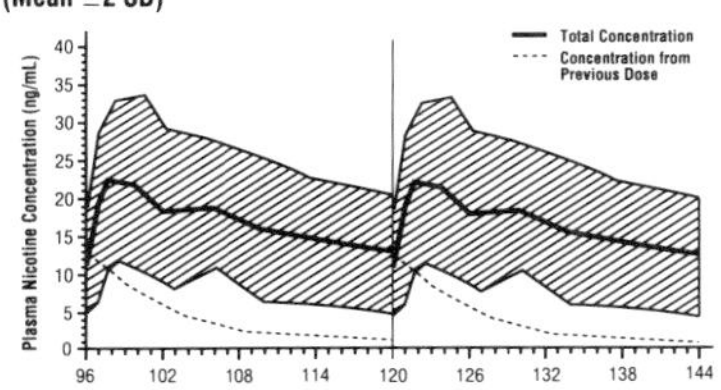

Following the second daily NICODERM system application, steady-state plasma nicotine concentrations are achieved and are on average 30% higher compared with single-dose applications. Plasma nicotine concentrations are proportional to dose (ie, linear kinetics are observed) for the three dosages of NICODERM systems. Nicotine kinetics are similar for all sites of application on the upper body and upper outer arm. Plasma nicotine concentrations from NICODERM 21 mg/day are the same as those from simultaneous use of NICODERM 14 mg/day and 7 mg/day.

Following removal of the NICODERM system, plasma nicotine concentrations decline in an exponential fashion with an apparent mean half-life of 3 to 4 hours (see dotted line in Figure) compared with 1 to 2 hours for IV administration, due to continued absorption from the skin depot. Most nonsmoking patients will have nondetectable nicotine concentrations in 10 to 12 hours.

Steady-State Nicotine Pharmacokinetic Parameters for Nicoderm Systems (Mean, SD, and Range)

	Dose Absorbed (mg/day) 21			14			7		
	Mean	SD	Range	Mean	SD	Range	Mean	SD	Range
C_{max} ng/mL	23	5	13-32	17	3	10-24	8	2	5-12
C_{avg} ng/mL	17	4	10-26	12	3	8-17	6	1	4-10
C_{min} ng/mL	11	3	6-17	7	2	4-11	4	1	3-6
T_{max} h	4	3	1-10	4	3	1-10	4	4	1-18

C_{max}: maximum observed plasma concentration
C_{avg}: average plasma concentration
C_{min}: minimum observed plasma concentration
T_{max}: time of maximum plasma concentration

Half-hourly smoking of cigarettes produces average plasma nicotine concentrations of approximately 44 ng/mL. In comparison, average plasma nicotine concentrations from NICODERM 21 mg/day are about 17 ng/mL.

There are no differences in nicotine kinetics between men and women using NICODERM systems. Linear regression of both AUC and C_{max} vs total body weight shows the expected inverse relationship. Obese men using NICODERM systems had significantly lower AUC and C_{max} values than normal weight men. Men and women having low body weight are expected to have higher AUC and C_{max} values.

CLINICAL STUDIES

The efficacy of NICODERM systems as an aid to smoking cessation was demonstrated in two placebo-controlled, double-blind trials of otherwise healthy patients (n = 756) smoking at least one pack of cigarettes per day. The trials consisted of 6 weeks of active treatment, 6 weeks of weaning off NICODERM systems, and 12 weeks of follow-up on no medication. Quitting was defined as total abstinence from smoking (as determined by patient diary and verified by expired carbon monoxide). The "quit rates" are the proportion of patients enrolled who abstained after week 2.

The two trials in otherwise healthy smokers showed that all NICODERM doses were more effective than placebo, and that treatment with NICODERM 21 mg/day for 6 weeks provided significantly higher quit rates than the 14 mg/day and placebo treatments at 6 weeks. Data from these two studies are combined in the Quit Rate table. Quit rates were still significantly different after an additional 6-week weaning period and at follow-up 3 months later. All patients were given weekly behavioral supportive care. As shown in the following table, the quit rates on each treatment varied 2- to 3-fold among clinics at 6 weeks.

Quit Rates After Week 2 According to Starting Dose
(N = 756 smokers in 9 clinics)

NICODERM Delivery Rate (mg/day)	Number of Patients	After 6 Weeks Range*	After Weaning Range*	At 6 Month Range*
21	249	32-92%	18-63%	3-50%
14	254	30-61%	15-52%	0-48%
Placebo	253	15-46%	0-38%	0-35%

*Range for 9 centers, number of patients per treatment ranged from 23-34

In a study of smokers with coronary artery disease, 77 patients treated with NICODERM systems (75% on 14 mg/day and 25% on 21 mg/day) had higher quit rates than 78 placebo-treated patients at the end of the 8-week study period (5 weeks of active treatment and 3 weeks of weaning). NICODERM systems did not affect angina frequency or the appearance of arrhythmias on Holter monitoring in these patients. Symptoms presumed related to nicotine withdrawal and the stress of smoking cessation caused more patients to terminate the study than symptoms thought to be related to nicotine substitution. Seven patients on placebo and one on NICODERM 14 mg/day dropped out for symptoms probably related to nicotine withdrawal (7 of these 8 patients experienced cardiovascular symptoms), while only two patients dropped out for nicotine-related symptoms (one patient with severe nausea on NICODERM 14 mg/day and one with nausea and palpitations on NICODERM 21 mg/day).

Patients who used NICODERM systems in clinical trials had a significant reduction in craving for cigarettes, a major nicotine withdrawal symptom, compared with placebo-treated patients (see Figure). Reduction in craving, as with quit rate, is quite variable. This variability is presumed to be due to inherent differences in patient populations (eg, patient motivation, concomitant illnesses, number of cigarettes smoked per day, number of years smoking, exposure to other smokers, socioeconomic status) as well as differences among the clinics.

Severity of Craving by Treatment From Clinical Trials (N = 877)

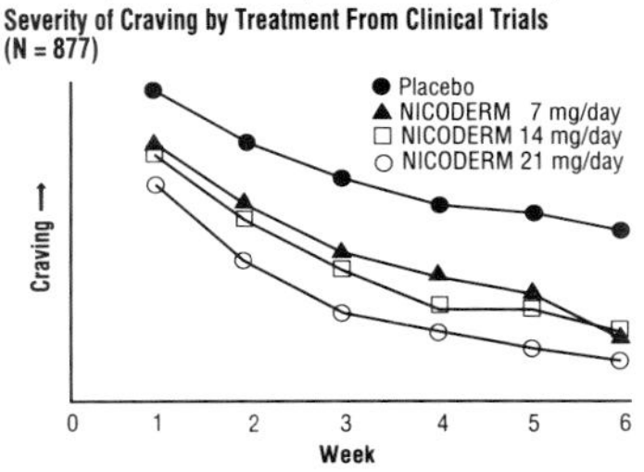

Patients using NICODERM systems dropped out of the trials less frequently than patients receiving placebo. Quit rates for the 56 patients over age 60 were comparable to the quit rates for the 821 patients aged 60 and under.

Individualization of Dosage

It is important to make sure that patients read the instructions made available to them and have their questions answered. They should clearly understand the directions for applying and disposing of NICODERM systems. They should be instructed to stop smoking completely when the first system is applied.

The success or failure of smoking cessation depends heavily on the quality, intensity, and frequency of supportive care. Patients are more likely to quit smoking if they are seen frequently and participate in formal smoking-cessation programs.

The goal of NICODERM therapy is complete abstinence. Significant health benefits have not been demonstrated for reduction of smoking. If a patient is unable to stop smoking by the fourth week of therapy, treatment should probably be discontinued. Patients who have not stopped smoking after 4 weeks of NICODERM therapy are unlikely to quit on that attempt.

Patients who fail to quit on any attempt may benefit from interventions to improve their chances for success on subsequent attempts. These patients should be counselled to determine why they failed and then probably be given a "therapy holiday" before the next attempt. A new quit attempt should be encouraged when the factors that contributed to failure can be eliminated or reduced, and conditions are more favorable.

Based on the clinical trials, a reasonable approach to assisting patients in their attempt to quit smoking is to assign their initial NICODERM treatment using the recommended dosing schedule (see Dosing Schedule below). The need for dose adjustment should be assessed during the first 2 weeks. Patients should continue the dose selected with counselling and support over the following month. Those who have successfully stopped smoking during that time should be supported during 4 to 8 weeks of weaning, after which treatment should be terminated.

Therapy generally should begin with the NICODERM 21 mg/day (see Dosing Schedule below) except if the patient is small (less than 100 pounds), is a light smoker (less than 1/2 pack of cigarettes per day), or has cardiovascular disease.

Dosing Schedule

	Otherwise Healthy Patients	Other* Patients
Initial/Starting Dose	21 mg/day	14 mg/day
Duration of Treatment	4-8 weeks	4-8 weeks
First Weaning Dose	14 mg/day	7 mg/day
Duration of Treatment	2-4 weeks	2-4 weeks
Second Weaning Dose	7 mg/day	
Duration of Treatment	2-4 weeks	

*Small patient (less than 100 pounds)
or light smoker (less than 10 cigarettes/day)
or patient with cardiovascular disease

The symptoms of nicotine withdrawal and excess overlap (see Pharmacodynamics and ADVERSE REACTIONS). Since patients using NICODERM systems may also smoke intermittently, it may be difficult to determine if patients are experiencing nicotine withdrawal or nicotine excess.

The controlled clinical trials using NICODERM therapy suggest that abnormal dreams and insomnia are more often symptoms of nicotine excess, while anxiety, somnolence, and depression are more often symptoms of nicotine withdrawal.

INDICATIONS AND USAGE

NICODERM treatment is indicated as an aid to smoking cessation for the relief of nicotine withdrawal symptoms. NICODERM treatment should be used as part of a comprehensive behavioral smoking-cessation program.
The use of NICODERM systems for longer than 3 months has not been studied.

CONTRAINDICATIONS

Use of NICODERM systems is contraindicated in patients with hypersensitivity or allergy to nicotine or to any of the components of the therapeutic system.

WARNINGS

Nicotine from any source can be toxic and addictive. Smoking causes lung cancer, heart disease, and emphysema and may adversely affect the fetus and the pregnant woman. For any smoker, with or without concomitant disease or pregnancy, the risk of nicotine replacement in a smoking-cessation program should be weighed against the hazard of continued smoking while using NICODERM systems and the likelihood of achieving cessation of smoking without nicotine replacement.

Pregnancy Warning

Tobacco smoke, which has been shown to be harmful to the fetus, contains nicotine, hydrogen cyanide, and carbon monoxide. Nicotine has been shown in animal studies to cause fetal harm. It is therefore presumed that NICODERM systems can cause fetal harm when administered to a pregnant woman. The effect of nicotine delivery by NICODERM systems has not been examined in pregnancy (see PRECAUTIONS).

Therefore pregnant smokers should be encouraged to attempt cessation using educational and behavioral interventions before using pharmacological approaches. If NICODERM systems are used during pregnancy, or if the patient becomes pregnant while using NICODERM systems, the patient should be apprised of the potential hazard to the fetus.

Safety Note Concerning Children

The amounts of nicotine that are tolerated by adult smokers can produce symptoms of poisoning and could prove fatal if the NICODERM system is applied or ingested by children or pets. Used 21 mg/day systems contain about 73% (83 mg) of their initial drug content. Therefore, patients should be cautioned to keep both the used and unused NICODERM systems out of the reach of children and pets.

PRECAUTIONS

The patient should be urged to stop smoking completely when initiating NICODERM therapy (see DOSAGE AND ADMINISTRATION). Patients should be informed that if they continue to smoke while using NICODERM systems, they may experience adverse effects due to peak nicotine levels higher than those experienced from smoking alone. If there is a clinically significant increase in cardiovascular or other effects attributable to nicotine, the NICODERM dose should be reduced or NICODERM treatment discontinued (see WARNINGS). Physicians should anticipate that concomitant medications may need dosage adjustment (see Drug Interactions).
The use of NICODERM systems beyond 3 months by patients who stop smoking should be discouraged, because the chronic consumption of nicotine by any route can be harmful and addicting.

Allergic Reactions

In a 6-week, open-label, dermal irritation and sensitization study of NICODERM systems, 7 of 230 patients exhibited definite erythema at 24 hours after application. Upon rechallenge, 4 patients exhibited mild to moderate contact allergy. Patients with contact sensitization should be cautioned that a serious reaction could occur from exposure to other nicotine-containing products or smoking. In the efficacy trials, erythema following system removal was typically seen in about 14% of patients, some edema in 3%, and dropouts due to skin reactions occurred in 2% of patients.
Patients should be instructed to promptly discontinue the use of NICODERM systems and contact their physicians, if they experience severe or persistent local skin reactions (eg, severe erythema, pruritus, or edema) at the site of application or a generalized skin reaction (eg, urticaria, hives, or generalized rash).
Patients using NICODERM therapy concurrently with other transdermal products may exhibit local reactions at both application sites. Reactions were seen in 2 of 7 patients using concomitant Estraderm® (estradiol transdermal system) in clinical trials. In such patients, use of one or both systems may have to be discontinued.

Skin Disease

NICODERM systems are usually well tolerated by patients with normal skin, but may be irritating for patients with some skin disorders (atopic or eczematous dermatitis).

Cardiovascular or Peripheral Vascular Diseases

The risks of nicotine replacement in patients with certain cardiovascular and peripheral vascular diseases should be weighed against the benefits of including nicotine replacement in a smoking-cessation program for them. Specifically, patients with coronary heart disease (history of myocardial infarction and/or angina pectoris), serious cardiac arrhythmias, or vasospastic diseases (Buerger's disease, Prinzmetal's variant angina) should be carefully screened and evaluated before nicotine replacement is prescribed.
Tachycardia occurring in association with the use of NICODERM therapy was reported occasionally. If serious cardiovascular symptoms occur with the use of NICODERM therapy, it should be discontinued.
NICODERM therapy was as well tolerated as placebo in a controlled trial in patients with coronary artery disease (see CLINICAL STUDIES). One patient on NICODERM 21mg/day, two on NICODERM 14 mg/day, and eight on placebo discontinued treatment due to adverse events.
NICODERM therapy did not affect angina frequency or the appearance of arrhythmias on Holter monitoring in these patients.
NICODERM therapy generally should not be used in patients during the immediate post-myocardial infarction period, patients with serious arrhythmias, and patients with severe or worsening angina pectoris.

Renal or Hepatic Insufficiency

The pharmacokinetics of nicotine have not been studied in the elderly or in patients with renal or hepatic impairment. However, given that nicotine is extensively metabolized and that its total system clearance is dependent on liver blood flow, some influence of hepatic impairment on drug kinetics (reduced clearance) should be anticipated. Only severe renal impairment would be expected to affect the clearance of nicotine or its metabolites from the circulation (see Pharmacokinetics).

Endocrine Diseases

NICODERM therapy should be used with caution in patients with hyperthyroidism, pheochromocytoma, or insulin-dependent diabetes, since nicotine causes the release of catecholamines by the adrenal medulla.

Peptic Ulcer Disease

Nicotine delays healing in peptic ulcer disease; therefore, NICODERM therapy should be used with caution in patients with active peptic ulcers and only when the benefits of including nicotine replacement in a smoking-cessation program outweigh the risks.

Accelerated Hypertension

Nicotine therapy constitutes a risk factor for development of malignant hypertension in patients with accelerated hypertension; therefore, NICODERM therapy should be used with caution in these patients and only when the benefits of including nicotine replacement in a smoking-cessation program outweigh the risks.

Information for Patient

A patient instruction booklet is included in the package of NICODERM systems dispensed to the patient. The instruction sheet contains important information and instructions on how to properly use and dispose of NICODERM systems. Patients should be encouraged to ask questions of the physician and pharmacist. Patients must be advised to keep both used and unused systems out of the reach of children and pets.

Drug Interactions

Smoking cessation, with or without nicotine replacement, may alter the pharmacokinetics of certain concomitant medications.

May Require a Decrease in Dose at Cessation of Smoking	Possible Mechanism
acetaminophen, caffeine, imipramine, oxazepam, pentazocine, propranolol, theophylline	Deinduction of hepatic enzymes on smoking cessation.
insulin	Increase in subcutaneous insulin absorption with smoking cessation.
adrenergic antagonists (eg, prazosin, labetalol)	Decrease in circulating catecholamines with smoking cessation.
May Require an Increase in Dose at Cessation of Smoking	**Possible Mechanism**
adrenergic agonists (eg, isoproterenol, phenylephrine)	Decease in circulating catecholamines with smoking cessation.

Carcinogenesis, Mutagenesis, Impairment of Fertility

Nicotine itself does not appear to be a carcinogen in laboratory animals. However, nicotine and its metabolites increased the incidences of tumors in the cheek pouches of hamsters and forestomach of F344 rats, respectively, when given in combination with tumor initiators. One study, which could not be replicated, suggested that cotinine, the primary metabolite of nicotine, may cause lymphoreticular sarcoma in the large intestine in rats.
Nicotine and cotinine were not mutagenic in the Ames *Salmonella* test. Nicotine induced repairable DNA damage in an *E. coli* test system. Nicotine was shown to be genotoxic in a test system using Chinese hamster ovary cells. In rats and rabbits, implantation can be delayed or inhibited by a reduction in DNA synthesis that appears to be caused by nicotine. Studies have shown a decrease in litter size in rats treated with nicotine during gestation.

Pregnancy

Pregnancy Category D (see WARNINGS).
The harmful effects of cigarette smoking on maternal and fetal health are clearly established. These include low birth weight, increased risk of spontaneous abortion, and increased perinatal mortality. The specific effects of NICODERM therapy on fetal development are unknown. Therefore pregnant smokers should be encouraged to attempt cessation using educational and behavioral interventions before using pharmacological approaches.
Spontaneous abortion during nicotine replacement therapy has been reported; as with smoking, nicotine as a contributing factor cannot be excluded.
NICODERM therapy should be used during pregnancy only if the likelihood of smoking cessation justifies the potential risk of use of nicotine replacement by the patient who may continue to smoke.

Teratogenicity

Animal Studies: Nicotine was shown to produce skeletal abnormalities in the offspring of mice when given doses toxic to the dams (25 mg/kg IP or SC).
Human Studies: Nicotine teratogenicity has not been studied in humans except as a component of cigarette smoke (each cigarette smoked delivers about 1 mg of nicotine). It has not been possible to conclude whether cigarette smoking is teratogenic to humans.

Other Effects

Animal Studies: A nicotine bolus (up to 2 mg/kg) to pregnant rhesus monkeys caused acidosis, hypercarbia, and hypotension (fetal and maternal concentrations were about 20 times those achieved after smoking 1 cigarette in 5 minutes). Fetal breathing movements were reduced in the fetal lamb after intravenous injection of 0.25 mg/kg nicotine to the ewe (equivalent to smoking 1 cigarette every 20 seconds for 5 minutes). Uterine blood flow was reduced about 30% after infusion of 0.1 mg/kg/min nicotine for 20 minutes to pregnant rhesus monkeys (equivalent to smoking about 6 cigarettes every minute for 20 minutes).
Human Experience: Cigarette smoking during pregnancy is associated with an increased risk of spontaneous abortion, low birth weight infants, and perinatal mortality. Nicotine and carbon monoxide are considered the most likely mediators of these outcomes. The effect of cigarette smoking on fetal cardiovascular parameters has been studied near term. Cigarettes increased fetal aortic blood flow and heart rate and decreased uterine blood flow and fetal breathing movements. NICODERM therapy has not been studied in pregnant humans.

Labor and Delivery

The NICODERM system is not recommended to be left on during labor and delivery. The effects of nicotine on a mother or the fetus during labor are unknown.

Use in Nursing Mothers

Caution should be exercised when NICODERM therapy is administered to nursing women. The safety of NICODERM therapy in nursing infants has not been examined. Nicotine passes freely into breast milk; the milk to plasma ratio averages 2.9. Nicotine is absorbed orally. An infant has the ability to clear nicotine by hepatic first-pass clearance; however, the efficiency of removal is probably lowest at birth. The nicotine concentrations in milk can be expected to be lower with NICODERM therapy, when used as directed, than with cigarette smoking, as maternal plasma nicotine concentrations are generally reduced with nicotine replacement. The risk of exposure of the infant to nicotine from NICODERM therapy should be weighed against the risks associated with the infant's exposure to nicotine from continued smoking by the mother (passive smoke exposure and contamination of breast milk with other components of tobacco smoke) and from NICODERM therapy alone or in combination with continued smoking.

Pediatric Use

NICODERM therapy is not recommended for use in children, because the safety and effectiveness of NICODERM therapy in children and adolescents who smoke have not been evaluated.

Geriatric Use

Fifty-six patients over the age of 60 participated in clinical trials of NICODERM therapy. NICODERM therapy appeared to be as effective in this age group as in younger smokers. However, asthenia, various body aches, and dizziness occurred slightly more often in patients over 60 years of age.

ADVERSE REACTIONS

Assessment of adverse events in the 1,131 patients who participated in controlled clinical trials is complicated by the occurrence of GI and CNS effects of nicotine withdrawal as well as nicotine excess. The actual incidences of both are confounded by concurrent smoking by many of the patients. When reporting adverse events during the trials, the investigators did not attempt to identify the cause of the symptom.

Topical Adverse Events

The most common adverse event associated with topical nicotine is a short-lived erythema, pruritus, and/or burning at the application site, which was seen at least once in 47% of patients on the NICODERM system in the clinical trials. Local erythema after system removal was noted at least once in 14% of patients and local edema in 3%. Erythema generally resolved within 24 hours. Cutaneous hypersensitivity (contact sensitization) occurred in 2% of patients on NICODERM systems (see PRECAUTIONS, Allergic Reactions).

Probably Causally Related

The following adverse events were reported more frequently in NICODERM-treated patients than in placebo-treated patients or exhibited a dose response in clinical trials.
Digestive System: Diarrhea*, dyspepsia*
Mouth/Tooth Disorders: Dry mouth†
Musculoskeletal System: Arthralgia†, myalgia*
Nervous System: Abnormal dreams*, insomnia (23%), nervousness*
Skin and Appendages: Sweating†

Frequencies for 21 mg/day system
* Reported in 3% to 9% of patients
† Reported in 1% to 3% of patients
Unmarked if reported in <1% of patients

Causal Relationship UNKNOWN

Adverse events reported in NICODERM- and placebo-treated patients at about the same frequency in clinical trials are listed below. The clinical significance of the association between NICODERM systems and these events is unknown, but they are reported as alerting information for the clinician.
Body as a Whole: Asthenia*, back pain*, chest pain†, pain*
Digestive System: Abdominal pain†, constipation*, nausea*, vomiting†
Nervous System: Dizziness*, headache (29%), paresthesia†
Respiratory System: Cough increased*, pharyngitis*, sinusitis†
Skin and Appendages: Rash*
Special Senses: Taste perversion*
Urogenital System: Dysmenorrhea*

Frequencies for 21 mg/day systems
*Reported in 3% to 9% of patients
†Reported in 1% to 3% of patients
Unmarked if reported in <1% of patients

DRUG ABUSE AND DEPENDENCE

NICODERM therapy is likely to have a low abuse potential based on differences between it and cigarettes in four characteristics commonly considered important in contributing to abuse: much slower absorption, much smaller fluctuations in blood levels, lower blood levels of nicotine, and less frequent use (ie, once daily).
Dependence on nicotine polacrilex chewing gum replacement therapy has been reported. Such dependence might also occur from transference to NICODERM systems of tobacco-based nicotine dependence. The use of the system beyond 3 months has not been evaluated and should be discouraged.
To minimize the risk of dependence, patients should be encouraged to withdraw gradually from NICODERM treatment after 4 to 8 weeks of use. Recommended dose reduction is to progressively decrease the dose every 2 to 4 weeks (see DOSAGE AND ADMINISTRATION).

OVERDOSAGE

The effects of applying several NICODERM systems simultaneously or swallowing NICODERM systems are unknown (see WARNINGS, Safety Note Concerning Children).
The oral LD_{50} for nicotine in rodents varies with species but is in excess of 24 mg/kg; death is due to respiratory paralysis. The oral minimum lethal dose of nicotine in dogs is greater than 5 mg/kg. The oral minimum acute lethal dose for nicotine in human adults is reported to be 40 to 60 mg (<1 mg/kg).
Three dogs, each weighing 11 kg, were fed two damaged NICODERM 14 mg/day systems. Nicotine plasma concentrations of 32 to 79 ng/mL were observed. No ill effects were apparent.
Signs and symptoms of an overdose from a NICODERM system would be expected to be the same as those of acute nicotine poisoning, including pallor, cold sweat, nausea, salivation, vomiting, abdominal pain, diarrhea, headache, dizziness, disturbed hearing and vision, tremor, mental confusion, and weakness. Prostration, hypotension, and respiratory failure may ensue with large overdoses. Lethal doses produce convulsions quickly, and death follows

as a result of peripheral or central respiratory paralysis or, less frequently, cardiac failure.

Overdose From Topical Exposure

The NICODERM system should be removed immediately if the patient shows signs of overdosage, and the patient should seek immediate medical care. The skin surface may be flushed with water and dried. No soap should be used, since it may increase nicotine absorption. Nicotine will continue to be delivered into the bloodstream for several hours (see Pharmacokinetics) after removal of the system because of a depot of nicotine in the skin.

Overdose From Ingestion

Persons ingesting NICODERM systems should be referred to a health care facility for management. Due to the possibility of nicotine-induced seizures, activated charcoal should be administered. In unconscious patients with a secure airway, instill activated charcoal via a nasogastric tube. A saline cathartic or sorbitol added to the first dose of activated charcoal may speed gastrointestinal passage of the system. Repeated doses of activated charcoal should be administered as long as the system remains in the gastrointestinal tract since it will continue to release nicotine for many hours.

Management of Nicotine Poisoning

Other supportive measures include diazepam or barbiturates for seizures, atropine for excessive bronchial secretions or diarrhea, respiratory support for respiratory failure, and vigorous fluid support for hypotension and cardiovascular collapse.

DOSAGE AND ADMINISTRATION

Patients must desire to stop smoking and should be instructed to stop smoking immediately as they begin using NICODERM therapy. The patient should read the patient instruction booklet on NICODERM therapy and be encouraged to ask any questions. Treatment should be initiated with NICODERM 21 mg/day or 14 mg/day systems (see Individualization of Dosage).

Once the appropriate dosage is selected the patient should begin 4 to 6 weeks of therapy at that dosage. The patient should stop smoking cigarettes completely during this period. If the patient is unable to stop cigarette smoking within 4 weeks, NICODERM therapy probably should be stopped, since few additional patients in clinical trials were able to quit after this time.

Recommended Dosing Schedule for Healthy Patients[a]
(See Individualization of Dosage)

Dose	Duration
NICODERM 21 mg/day	First 6 Weeks
NICODERM 14 mg/day	Next 2 Weeks[b]
NICODERM 7 mg/day	Last 2 Weeks[c]

[a] Start with NICODERM 14 mg/day for 6 weeks for patients who:
- have cardiovascular disease
- weigh less than 100 pounds
- smoke less than 1/2 a pack of cigarettes/day

Decrease dose to NICODERM 7 mg/day for the final 2-4 weeks.

[b] Patients who have successfully abstained from smoking should have their dose of NICODERM reduced after each 2-4 weeks of treatment until the 7 mg/day dose has been used for 2-4 weeks (see Individualization of Dosage).

[c] The entire course of nicotine substitution and gradual withdrawal should take 8-12 weeks, depending on the size of the initial dose. The use of NICODERM systems beyond 3 months has not been studied.

The NICODERM system should be applied promptly upon its removal from the protective pouch to prevent evaporative loss of nicotine from the system. NICODERM systems should be used only when the pouch is intact to assure that the product has not been tampered with.

NICODERM systems should be applied only once a day to a non-hairy, clean, dry skin site on the upper body or upper outer arm. After 24 hours, the used NICODERM system should be removed and a new system applied to an alternate skin site. Skin sites should not be reused for at least a week. Patients should be cautioned not to continue to use the same system for more than 24 hours.

SAFETY AND HANDLING

The NICODERM system can be a dermal irritant and can cause contact sensitization. Patients should be instructed in the proper use of NICODERM systems by using demonstration systems. Although exposure of health care workers to nicotine from NICODERM systems should be minimal, care should be taken to avoid unnecessary contact with active systems. If you do handle active systems, wash with water alone, since soap may increase nicotine absorption. Do not touch your eyes.

Disposal

When the used system is removed from the skin, it should be folded over and placed in the protective pouch that contained the new system. The used system should be immediately disposed of in such a way to prevent its access by children or pets. See patient information for further directions on handling and disposal.

How Supplied

See DESCRIPTION for total nicotine content per unit.

NDC 0088-0050-61
NICODERM 21 mg/day, 14 systems per box
NDC 0088-0051-61
NICODERM 14 mg/day, 14 systems per box
NDC 0088-0052-61
NICODERM 7 mg/day, 14 systems per box

How to Store

Do not store above 86°F (30°C) because NICODERM systems are sensitive to heat. A slight discoloration of the system is not significant.

Do not store unpouched. Once removed from the protective pouch, NICODERM systems should be applied promptly, since nicotine is volatile and the systems may lose strength.

CAUTION: Federal law prohibits dispensing without prescription.

Manufactured by
ALZA Corporation
Palo Alto, CA 94304 for
Marion Merrell Dow Inc.
Kansas City, MO 64114

Prescribing Information as of January 1992
nidp0192n

PATIENT INSTRUCTIONS

NICODERM®
(nicotine transdermal system)
IMPORTANT

YOUR DOCTOR HAS PRESCRIBED THIS DRUG FOR YOUR USE ONLY. DO NOT LET ANYONE ELSE USE IT.

KEEP THIS MEDICINE OUT OF THE REACH OF CHILDREN AND PETS. Nicotine can be very toxic and harmful. Small amounts of nicotine can cause serious illness in children. Even used NICODERM patches contain enough nicotine to poison children and pets. Be sure to throw away NICODERM patches out of the reach of children and pets. If a child puts on or plays with a NICODERM patch that is out of its sealed pouch, take it away from the child and contact a poison control center or a doctor immediately.

Women. Nicotine in any form may cause harm to your unborn baby, if you use nicotine while you are pregnant. Do not use NICODERM patches if you are pregnant or nursing unless advised by your doctor. If you become pregnant while using NICODERM patches, or if you think you might be pregnant, stop smoking and don't use NICODERM patches until you have talked to your doctor.

This leaflet will provide you with general information about nicotine and specific instructions about how to use NICODERM patches. It is important that you read it carefully and completely before you start using NICODERM patches. Be sure to read the PRECAUTIONS section before using NICODERM patches, because as with all drugs, NICODERM patches have side effects. Since this leaflet is only a summary of information, be sure to ask your doctor if you have any questions or want to know more.

Marion Merrell Dow has developed "The 6-2-2 Committed Quitter's Program," which gives you useful tips on how to quit smoking while using NICODERM patches. If you do not have a copy, please ask your doctor or pharmacist about it. They can order it for you, or you can call for it yourself at 1-800-835-5634. There is no charge for the 6-2-2 Committed Quitter's Program.

INTRODUCTION

IT IS IMPORTANT THAT YOU ARE FIRMLY COMMITTED TO GIVING UP SMOKING.

NICODERM is a skin patch containing nicotine designed to help you quit smoking cigarettes. When you wear a NICODERM patch, it releases nicotine through the skin into your bloodstream while you are wearing it. The nicotine that is in your skin will still be entering your bloodstream for several hours after you take the patch off.

It is the nicotine in cigarettes that causes addiction to smoking. The NICODERM patch replaces some of the nicotine you crave when you are stopping smoking. The NICODERM patch may also help relieve other symptoms of nicotine withdrawal that may occur when you stop smoking such as irritability, frustration, anger, anxiety, difficulty in concentration, and restlessness.

There are three doses of NICODERM patches. Your doctor has chosen the dose of the NICODERM patch you are using and may adjust it during the first week or two. After about 6 weeks, your doctor will give you smaller NICODERM patches approximately every 2 weeks. The smaller patches give you less nicotine. In time, you will be completely off nicotine.

INFORMATION ABOUT NICODERM PATCHES

How the NICODERM Patch Works

NICODERM patches contain nicotine. When you put a NICODERM patch on your skin, nicotine passes from the patch through the skin and into your blood.

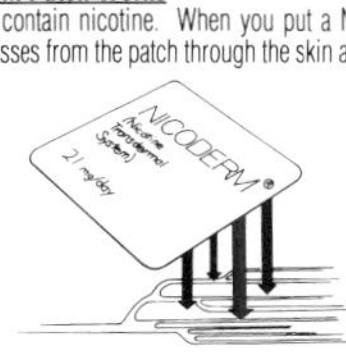

How to Apply NICODERM Patches

Step 1. Choose a non-hairy, clean, dry area of your front or back above the waist or the upper outer part of your arm. Do not put NICODERM patches on skin that is burned, broken out, cut, or irritated in any way.

Step 2. Do not remove the NICODERM patch from its sealed protective pouch until you are ready to use it. NICODERM patches will lose nicotine to the air if you store them out of the pouch. Before putting on the patch, tear open the pouch. Do not use scissors to open the pouch because you might accidentally cut the patch. Discard the used patch you take off by putting it in the pouch that you take the new patch out of. The used patch should be thrown away in the trash out of the reach of children and pets (see Step 7).

Step 3. A stiff, clear, protective liner covers the sticky silver side of the NICODERM patch—the side that will be put on your skin. The liner has a slit down the middle to help you remove it from the patch. With the silver side facing you, pull one half of the liner away from the NICODERM patch starting at the middle slit. Hold the NICODERM patch at one of the outside edges (touch the sticky side as little as possible), and pull off the other half of the protective liner. Throw away this liner.

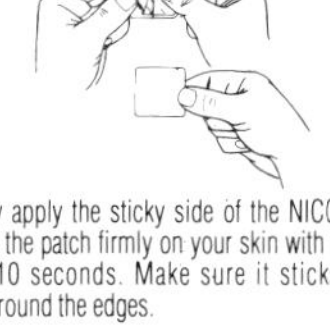

Step 4. Immediately apply the sticky side of the NICODERM patch to your skin. Press the patch firmly on your skin with the palm of your hand for about 10 seconds. Make sure it sticks well to your skin, especially around the edges.

Step 5. Wash your hands when you have finished applying the NICODERM patch. Nicotine on your hands could get into your eyes and nose and could cause stinging, redness, or more serious problems.

Step 6. After approximately 24 hours, remove the patch you have been wearing. Choose a different place on your skin to apply the next NICODERM patch and repeat Steps 1 to 5. Do not return to a previously used skin site for at least one week. Do not leave on the NICODERM patch for more than 24 hours because it may irritate your skin and because it also loses strength after 24 hours.

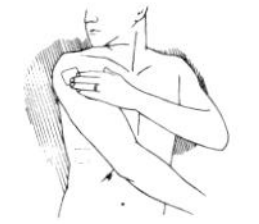

Step 7. Fold the used NICODERM patch in half with the silver side together. After you have put on a new patch, take its pouch and place the used folded NICODERM patch inside of it. Throw the pouch in the trash away from children and pets.

When to Apply NICODERM Patches

Applying the NICODERM patch at about the same time each day will help you to remember when to put on a new NICODERM patch. If you want to change the time when you put on your patch, you can do so. Just remove the NICODERM patch you are wearing and put on a new one. After that, apply the NICODERM patch at the new time each day.

If Your NICODERM Patch Gets Wet

Water will not harm the NICODERM patch you are wearing. You can bathe, swim, use the hot tub, or shower while you are wearing the NICODERM patch.

If Your NICODERM Patch Comes Off

If your NICODERM patch falls off, put on a new one. Remove the NICODERM patch at your regular time to keep your schedule the same or 24 hours after applying the replacement patch if you wish to change the time each day that you apply a new patch. Before putting on a new patch, make sure you select a non-hairy area that is not irritated and that is clean and dry.

Disposing of NICODERM Patches

Fold the used patch in half with the silver side together. After you put on a new NICODERM patch, take its opened pouch or aluminum foil and place the used folded NICODERM patch inside of it. THROW THE POUCH IN THE TRASH AWAY FROM CHILDREN AND PETS.

Storage Instructions

Keep each NICODERM patch in its protective pouch until you are ready to use it, because the patch will lose nicotine into the air if it's outside the pouch. Do not store NICODERM patches above 86°F (30°C) because they are sensitive to heat. Remember, the inside of your car can reach temperatures much higher than this in the summer.

PRECAUTIONS

What to Ask Your Doctor

Ask your doctor about possible problems with NICODERM patches. Be sure to tell your doctor if you have had any of the following:

- a recent heart attack (myocardial infarction)
- irregular heart beat (arrhythmia)
- severe or worsening heart pain (angina pectoris)
- allergies to drugs
- rashes from adhesive tape or bandages
- skin diseases
- very high blood pressure
- stomach ulcers
- overactive thyroid
- diabetes requiring insulin
- kidney or liver disease

If You Are Taking Medicines

NICODERM treatment, together with stopping smoking, may change the effect of other medicines. It is important to tell your doctor about all the medicines you are taking.

What to Watch For (Adverse Effects)

You should not smoke while using the NICODERM patch. It is possible to get too much nicotine (an overdose), especially if you use the NICODERM patch and smoke at the same time. Signs of an overdose include bad headaches, dizziness, upset stomach, drooling, vomiting, diarrhea, cold sweat, blurred vision, difficulty with hearing, mental confusion, and weakness. An overdose might cause you to faint.

If Your Skin Reacts to the NICODERM Patch

When you first put on a NICODERM patch, mild itching, burning, or tingling is normal and should go away within an hour. After you remove a NICODERM patch, the skin under the patch might be somewhat red. Your skin should not stay red for more than a day. If you get a skin rash after using a NICODERM patch, or if the skin under the patch becomes swollen or very red, call your doctor. Do not put on a new patch. You may be allergic to one of the components of the NICODERM patch. If you do become allergic to the nicotine in the NICODERM patch, you could get sick from using cigarettes or other nicotine-containing products.

What to Do When Problems Occur

IF YOU NOTICE ANY WORRISOME SYMPTOMS OR PROBLEMS, TAKE OFF THE NICODERM PATCH AND CALL YOUR DOCTOR AT ONCE.

Edward C. Lynch, M.D.
Associate Chairman
Department of Medicine
The Methodist Hospital
6535 Fannin - M. S. B - 501
Houston, Texas 77030